CONTENTS

PLAGUES

AND THEIR

AFTERMATH

PLAGUES
AND THEIR
AFTERMATH

*How Societies
Recover
from Pandemics*

**BRIAN MICHAEL
JENKINS**

MELVILLE HOUSE
BROOKLYN • LONDON

Plagues and Their Aftermath

First published in 2022 by Melville House
Copyright © Brian Michael Jenkins 2022
All rights reserved
First Melville House Printing: September 2022

Melville House Publishing
46 John Street
Brooklyn, NY 11201
and
Melville House UK
Suite 2000
16/18 Woodford Road
London E7 0HA

mhpbooks.com
@melvillehouse

ISBN: 978-1-68589-016-2
ISBN: 978-1-68589-017-9 (eBook)

Library of Congress Control Number: 2022938593

Designed by Emily Considine

Printed in the United States of America

10 9 8 7 6 5 4 3 2 1

A catalog record for this book is available
from the Library of Congress

AUTHOR'S NOTE

MY USUAL FIELD of analysis is political violence and irregular warfare. Therefore, it was not surprising that, on a number of occasions during the COVID-19 pandemic, I was asked how COVID-19 might affect terrorism. Would the pandemic suppress terrorist activity? Or would it inspire higher levels of political violence? Would it encourage terrorists to employ biological weapons? Would it start wars?

Proceeding directly from a pandemic (by definition a phenomenon of global proportions) to terrorism (a particular form of political violence) seems like reversing the sequence often cited in discussions of catastrophe theory. Instead of imagining how the flutter of a butterfly's wings might set off a string of events that escalate to a hurricane, we are attempting to imagine how a hurricane might affect the future flight patterns of butterflies. Clearly, however, pandemics have profound effects on society, creating new political tensions which, in turn, may lead to violence. We are already seeing that.

In the late summer of 2020, Professor Nicolas Stockhammer at the University of Vienna asked me if I would be willing to write a chapter on the topic of terrorism during and after the pandemic for a book being produced by the European Institute for Counter Terrorism and Conflict Prevention.[1] I agreed, and in the following months of shutdowns, social distancing, and no travel, my collection of books on the history of past epidemics grew steadily. I finished my chapter for the book, but I was increasingly fascinated with the subject of plagues in general—including the economic, societal, psychological, and political effects of major outbreaks of disease—and I kept going.

The myriad effects of past pandemics provide clues to understanding the possible consequences of the current pandemic. The results related here are still speculative but, I hope, are instructive.

Today's pandemic will eventually fade—we are not sure how or when that will take place—but the normality we knew before will not return. What the post-pandemic world will look like is far from clear. Uncertainty may be its dominant feature. It is therefore important that we think about, even speculatively, possible shifts in and potential shocks to our economic structures, political landscape, and even mass psychology. Physicians talk about "long COVID," the range of ongoing, recurring, or new medical conditions that can appear long after the initial infection; the concept has a broader application to society as a whole.

INTRODUCTION

And, as the story plain doth tell,
within the Countrey there did rest
A dredfull Dragon, fierce and fell,
whereby they were full sore opprest:
Who by his poisoned breath each day
did many of the City slay.

—THE SHIRBURN BALLADS, 1585–1616.

EARLY CHRONICLERS CONNECTED plagues with pestilential fumes from fire-breathing dragons.[1] The idea, although fanciful, was not far from medical theory at the time, which attributed outbreaks of disease to miasmas—concentrations of poisonous vapors. Although contagion theory replaced noxious-air explanations of infirmity in the nineteenth century, as late as the mid-1960s, when I was a soldier in the Dominican Republic, farmers showing up at our makeshift medical clinic still blamed chronic aches and other health problems on "a bad wind" ("*un viento malo*") that had entered their body, usually at night.

The focus in this study is not on the causes of epidemics but on their consequences. Like dragons, epidemics have long, thrashing tails—legacies not only of lives lost but of devastated economies and social disorder. These, in turn, are likely to have political repercussions. The COVID-19 pandemic will be intensively studied, but it may be years before its effects can be observed and analyzed. Past epidemics, however, offer clues as to what could occur in a future post-pandemic environment.

Scholars have produced a rich literature of past outbreaks of disease, ranging from Thucydides' account of the plague that ravaged Athens starting in 430 B.C.E. to recent accounts of the AIDS and Ebola epidemics.[2]

The effects of epidemics are not measured only in mortality. "Their secondary consequences," a prominent bacteriologist wrote in 1934, "have been much more far-reaching and disorganizing than anything that could have resulted from the mere reduction of the population."[3]

Secondary effects include the economic and social disruptions caused by the contagion and efforts to contain it, the effects of widespread fear and public hysteria, increased suspicion and scapegoating, the spread of rumors and conspiracy theories, and political disturbances and disorder that undermine government legitimacy. Modern medicine has been able to reduce the number of deaths and to mitigate, if not eliminate, the sense of helplessness and despair that people must have felt in previous centuries when faced with plagues they could not understand.[4] With advances in science able to reduce mortality—especially as a percentage of the world's population, other kinds of disruptions may now be the primary effects of epidemics.

Historical descriptions of the impact of epidemics fall into several broad categories. Traditional historians relating the history of a country or people mention epidemics only when the epidemics clearly alter the trajectory of events—for example, when they result in the loss of a war, contribute to the fall of an empire, or have such dramatic depopulation effects that they change the organization of society.

More recent historians look at huge swaths of time and territory to uncover underlying forces that affect the course of events in ways that conventional national histories might miss. As Jared Diamond noted in *Guns, Germs, and Steel*, "Because diseases have been the biggest killers of people, they have been decisive shapers of history."[5]

Disease has also attracted a set of historians who see epidemics as a distinct category for analysis. As Frank Snowden wrote in *Epidemics and Society*, "Epidemics have left a particular legacy in their wake. Their singularity merits attention."[6] Historians of epidemics analyze the effects of various contagious diseases throughout history or document specific outbreaks of disease and their consequences in certain regions, countries, or cities. With its massive death toll, Europe's Black Death of the fourteenth century has probably attracted the most attention, but books such as *Death in Hamburg, Naples in the Time of Cholera,* or *Russia and the Cholera: 1823–1832,* cited above, provide detailed accounts of the social and political effects of other epidemics.

In this book, we look at the plagues that afflicted the last centuries of the Roman Empire, the Black Death that ravaged Europe in the Middle Ages and returned in waves over the next four hundred years, the cholera epidemics that washed back and forth across Europe during the nineteenth and early twentieth centuries, the third pandemic of the bubonic plague in the late nineteenth century, and the 1918 "Spanish" flu pandemic that killed between 50 and 100 million people worldwide.[7] Outbreaks of smallpox, typhus, yellow fever, AIDS, Ebola, and other mass killers are also discussed. (A *dramatis pestilentiae* is provided at the end of the book.)

These historical examples serve as a template for identifying recurring attributes of post-epidemic history. Taking a thematic rather than a chronological or geographical approach, this study catalogs the immediate effects of epidemics and examines the potential longer-term repercussions of today's ongoing COVID-19 pandemic.

We begin by comparing the human toll of the COVID-19 pandemic with the mortality of past epidemics. We then compare the responses to previous outbreaks of disease with the immediately observable economic and societal effects of the current pandemic. The discussion next examines the possible political consequences of COVID-19. The longer-term effects are necessarily speculative—historians still debate the consequences of the Black Death, which began nearly seven centuries ago.

Finally, we explore how past epidemics have affected armed conflict and whether the COVID-19 pandemic might promote future wars or terrorist campaigns or encourage the use of biological weapons. A concluding section summarizes the observations.

The COVID-19 pandemic is by definition a global event, and this analysis is intended to be global in its scope. The United States admittedly dominates the narrative for several reasons. As we are dealing with a fast-moving topic, a greater volume of information regarding the United States was available to me. It is also true that, according to the latest reported statistics (April 2022), the United States not only leads the world in the total number of reported cases but accounts for more than 16 percent of the world's total.[8] With no intention of marginalizing other countries, I have greater familiarity with the social and political situation in the United States. Others will be able to offer more informed comments on the economic, social, and political developments in their countries, making international comparisons possible.

This is a preliminary work. As of April 2022, the COVID-19 pandemic is still not contained, making all conclusions tentative. While the virus is declining in some countries, it is surging in many others. Its impact will vary from region to region, country to country, city to city. Mutations of the virus, some more contagious or having greater effect on younger people, have been identified. A fifth wave, involving the Omicron variant of the virus, spread throughout the world and then subsided, but a further variant reported in March 2022 reversed the downward trend of cases in a number of countries. At the same time, China and Hong Kong, which had managed to quickly suppress the contagion in early 2020 through strict lockdowns, saw a sharp rise in cases.[9] Still more variants will no doubt appear. We are uncertain yet if efforts to slow the spread of the virus, combined with vaccination efforts, will bring the pandemic to an end, much as the 1918 flu outbreak ended, or if instead the virus will become endemic as waves of new variants wash back and forth across the planet. Are we looking at recovery, or at a new and chronic human condition?

CHAPTER 1:
THE HUMAN TOLL

THE MAGNITUDE OF death is a key factor in determining the scale and nature of an epidemic's impact on society. Obviously, it makes a difference whether an epidemic kills 0.5 percent or 2 percent of a given population and whether the outbreak affects an entire continent or a single city. But while the death toll would seem to be the easiest attribute to measure and compare, it turns out to be very difficult to quantify.

Accurate counts of the dead are unavailable for outbreaks of disease that occurred centuries ago. Local parish records, where obtainable, are fairly reliable sources for limited localities, but they cannot easily be extrapolated, since even rampant epidemics like the Black Death affected populations unevenly. For national or larger regional totals, we have at best only estimates.

The impact of an epidemic also varies according to its duration. High death tolls can reflect rapid depopulation caused by the disease, or an accumulation of deaths over a long period of time. Between the years 1347 and 1351, the first wave of the bubonic plague, or Black Death, killed between 25 and 50 million people in Europe—as much as half of the continent's population. Lesser outbreaks continued. By the mid-seventeenth century, when the plague began to decline, it had killed between 75 and 100 million people.

The 1918 flu pandemic killed 50 to 100 million people in 1918–1919 (including an estimated 675,000 in the United States). The AIDS virus has killed between 26 and 42 million people so far, but fatalities from AIDS have been spread over a period of nearly forty years since the early 1980s (about 700,000 AIDS deaths have occurred in the United States). Smallpox killed an estimated 300 to 500 million people in the twentieth century until 1980, when the United Nations World Health Organization (WHO) officially declared it eradicated.

The death toll of pandemics can be expressed not only in numbers but as a percentage of the total population. Epidemics are measured against local populations, whereas pandemics are often compared with the global population—although they may not affect the entire world, and world population estimates before the early modern era were sketchy.

The Antonine Plague, named so because it appeared during the reign of the Roman emperor Marcus Aurelius Antoninus Augustus, occurred between 165 and 180 C.E. It was brought back from the Middle East by Roman soldiers and spread quickly throughout the Roman Empire, killing an estimated 5 million people. This represented no more than a small percentage of the estimated world population of the time. The Justinian Plague, which occurred during the reign of the Byzantine emperor Justinian I, began in 541–542, but persisted for two hundred years and is considered the third-worst epidemic in history, eventually killing an estimated 25 to 50 million people (some say 30 to 100 million)—possibly 15 percent or more of the world's population at the time, but a full half of the population of Europe.[1]

Assuming the global population to have been somewhere around 375 million in the mid-fourteenth century, the 25 to 50 million deaths caused by the first wave of the Black Death would represent no more than 15 percent of the world's population, but between a third and two-thirds of Europe's population at the time, perhaps more.[2] An important caveat, however: Both the estimated death tolls and world population figures through the Middle Ages are no more than educated guesses.

According to a conservative estimate, the third major plague pandemic—which began in Yunnan Province in China in 1855, reaching Hong Kong in 1894 and from there spreading to India—killed an estimated 15 to 20 million people, less than 2 percent of the world's population at the time.[3]

Local populations, especially in crowded cities where outbreaks occurred, could be gravely affected. Thucydides, in his account of the Peloponnesian War fought between Athens and Sparta in the fifth century B.C.E., described in detail the devastating effects of the plague that struck Athens.[4] Plague in Florence in the 1340s killed half of the city's population.[5] Only a quarter of Barcelona's population reportedly survived the first year of the Black Death.[6] Many small European towns and villages disappeared altogether. Other towns and villages sealed themselves from outsiders and survived.

The intensity of epidemics also varies according to the

velocity, duration, and persistence of the disease over time. The record of past epidemics is sobering. We tend to think of epidemics as finite events of relatively short duration, but that has rarely been the case. The Justinian Plague began with an intense outbreak of bubonic plague that lasted from 541 to 549. This was only the first of fifteen or more waves that lasted until the year 750 before subsiding. The disease was caused by *Yersinia pestis*, a bacterium spread by fleas hosted by small mammals, primarily rats, that infested ancient and medieval cities. When the rats died, the fleas jumped to other hosts, including humans. The *Y. pestis* infection appeared in two forms: bubonic plague, which manifested itself in swollen, black lymph nodes (hence the name "Black Death"), and pneumonic plague, which moved into the lungs.

The first wave of the Black Death, which lasted several years, was sudden and devastating, but the plague was also persistent and it returned in at least seventeen more localized waves over the next three centuries. In 1665, a round of bubonic plague killed more than 100,000 inhabitants of London in eight months. Cholera washed across the world in seven successive waves during the nineteenth and early twentieth centuries.

In contrast, the 1918 influenza pandemic infected about a third of the world's population in just two years, but it then faded as people developed immunity. Years later, however, its viral descendants combined with other flu strains to create the 1957 Asian flu, the 1968 Hong Kong flu, the 1977 Russian flu, and the 2009 swine flu.[7]

In addition to the major killers—bubonic and pneumonic plague, smallpox, pandemic influenza, cholera—there are a host of other diseases, including epidemic typhus, yellow fever, and Ebola, which normally have more localized effects. The tolls from these may not rise to the levels seen in the Black Death or even the 1918 flu pandemic, but they can sometimes produce very high death counts. Between 1917 and 1921, typhus, which historically is often associated with wars and troop concentrations, killed as many as 3 million people in Russia. Still more people died of the disease in Eastern Europe and the Balkans during the same period.[8] Typhus, which was also called "the Hungarian disease," often accompanied other epidemics, adding to the death toll. During the Thirty Years' War (1618–1648), starvation, plague, and typhus killed an estimated 10 million people, while 350,000 were killed in combat. Typhus was dominant during the first half of the war, and plague deaths dominated the second half.[9]

Improved sanitation and modern medicine have reduced the death tolls of the more recent epidemics. But the time required to understand a new disease, then develop, manufacture, and distribute vaccines in sufficient quantities to cover the world's nearly 8 billion people—and to persuade those people to accept the vaccines—gives new viruses a head start.

Looking at the currently continuing surges of COVID-19, experts believe that eradicating the virus across the globe is unlikely. New mutations will continue to appear. Containing new outbreaks may be possible, but a more likely scenario is cohabitation. Essentially, that means accepting the virus as a more dangerous version of the ordinary flu. Recurring control measures and annual vaccinations to cover new variants should slow the disease's spread and minimize the death toll. Conceivably, we could see the development of even more effective vaccines that prevent transmission of new variants, or of an efficacious antiviral drug that prevents serious illness.

The worst-case scenario would be what scientists have called "conflagration," which would see new surges driven by ever more contagious or lethal variants.[10] Even without ascending to the death tolls of history's earlier epidemics, cohabitation with or a conflagration of COVID-19 would have profound effects on the economy, society, and individual behavior.

Finally, the impact of mass deaths in any society varies according to how epidemics compare with other causes of death and prevailing life expectancy at the time, which differ according to the economic standing of the victims. Famine, disease, wars, and inadequate medical care limited average life expectancy in Western nations to thirty to forty years until the nineteenth century, but class distinctions made a difference—lords lived far longer than peasants. This is not to say that dramatic increases in mortality had little effect on mindset and behavior in societies where many died young. But contemporary societies may be more sensitive to sudden increases in mortality than earlier societies were.

Are today's sensitivities causing people to exaggerate the pandemic? Some might say so, but the numbers suggest that the COVID-19 pandemic is likely to enter the ranks of the great calamities of the modern era.

We do not yet know what the final death toll of the COVID-19 pandemic will be. Globally recorded fatalities will surpass 6 million and, according to current projections, could reach 7 million by late summer of 2022.[11] Estimates of excess deaths resulting from the pandemic run above 18 million. There also may be upward revisions as more data become available.

The 1918 flu pandemic killed an estimated 50 to 100 million people in 1918 and 1919. The upper figure would make it the worst calamity in recent centuries in terms of total deaths. World War II (1939–1945) remains the deadliest modern event: six years of total war resulted in 60 to 85 million deaths.[12] Anywhere between 20 and 50 million people died during the 1959–1961 famine in China; it is considered the largest famine in human history.[13] Estimates of the number of total deaths from AIDS run between 26 and 42 million—the United Nations uses 36 million as its estimate—but these deaths occurred over nearly four decades.[14] The 1907 famine in China brought 25 million deaths.[15] Between 20 and 25 million people died in the Second Sino-Japanese War (1937–1945). An estimated 18 to 20 million died in World War I (1914–1918). The third plague pandemic (1855–1902) killed an estimated 15 to 20 million. Between 8 and 12 million people died in the Chinese Civil War (1927–1949). As noted above, more than 6 million COVID-19 deaths have been recorded worldwide, but estimates of excess deaths caused by the pandemic run two to four times that number. That would give us a potential total death toll of somewhere between 12 and 24 million, putting the COVID-19 pandemic at seventh place on the list of modern calamities.[16] Undeniably, it is already a large-scale human tragedy.

The COVID-19 pandemic has resulted in the greatest decline in annual life expectancy in the United States since World War II. The life expectancy of the average American decreased by 1.8 years in 2020.[17] Only the year before, the country had slightly rebounded from a tilt downward caused by the opioid epidemic and a dramatic increase in suicides. In contrast, the 1918 flu pandemic, which resulted in high mortality among younger people, had a much greater effect on life expectancy in the United States, reducing it by approximately 12 years.[18]

The effects of COVID-19 on the life expectancy of different sections of American society are unequal. Reporting early in the pandemic indicated that life expectancy for Hispanics declined by 1.8 years, and that of African Americans declined by 2.7 years, versus a decline of 0.8 years for white Americans.[19] This may leave a legacy of resentment in some segments of society that have suffered disproportionately. By February 2022, the racial disparities in cases and death rates had narrowed. Hispanics suffered a larger share of cases relative to their share of the total population while their share of deaths was close to their share of the population. Blacks suffered a similar share of the cases compared to their share of the population, but slightly more deaths. Whites suffered fewer cases than their share of the population, but a larger share of deaths, principally reflecting the Omicron surge beginning in late 2021. However, when adjusted for age, which is important because the risks of hospitalization and death increase with age, the racial and ethnic disparities remained significant—Blacks, Hispanics, American Indians, and Alaska Natives were about twice as likely to die from COVID-19 as white people.[20]

The COVID-19 pandemic thus far appears to be killing fewer people than the great pandemics of history, especially in proportion to the world's growing population. We are fortunate in having recent advances in science and medicine. Without vaccines, modern drugs, intensive-care treatment, and respiratory therapy, the world would be back where it was at the time of the 1918 flu pandemic and the COVID-19 death toll would be much higher. We can get a rough idea of how much higher by looking at the example of Peru, where the virus overwhelmed the country's weak health-care system. As of April 2022, Peru had recorded more than 3.5 million cases of COVID-19, which resulted in 212,486 deaths. Fatalities occurred in just under 6 percent of the cases. Extrapolating that ratio to the approximately 500 million cases recorded worldwide would result in a global death toll of nearly 30 million instead of 6 million (although again, COVID-19 deaths are probably undercounted). This is roughly 60 percent of the 1918 flu's lower estimated death toll, which was about 50 million. However, the world's population was much smaller in the early 1900s, so the percentage of fatalities caused by the 1918 pandemic was much higher.

As of April 2022, more than a million COVID-19 deaths had been recorded in the United States.[21] If Peru's higher mortality rate were applied to the total number of U.S. cases, the number of deaths in the United States would have been more than 4.9 million.

Celebrations may be inappropriate while a deadly pandemic continues to rage, but the number of lives saved as a result of modern medicine and the valiant work of health professionals is a remarkable achievement that should be kept in mind as one hears daily of science being dismissed, while public health officials, physicians, and health workers are disparaged and sometimes physically assaulted.

The number of deaths related to COVID-19 is probably underreported. Statistics from many developing countries are not considered accurate. The official death toll in India, for example, reportedly may reflect only a fraction of the total number of deaths in that country.[22] Many who die of COVID-19 are never tested for it. Other deaths could have been prevented if hospitals were not filled with COVID-19 patients. Even in the economically more advanced nations, undercounts may result from the way deaths are recorded. Excess deaths—a number beyond what would be statistically predicted on the basis of past trends—may provide more accurate totals than counts of deaths listed specifically as due to COVID-19. Excess deaths, however, can be calculated in a variety of ways—the math gets complicated.

Excess deaths can include deaths listed as caused only by the COVID-19 infection plus deaths resulting from respiratory, circulatory, or other prevalent conditions where COVID-19 is also listed as a cause. According to a study early in the pandemic done by the U.S. Centers for Disease Control and Prevention (CDC), as of the end of April 2021, estimated excess deaths related to COVID-19 were anywhere from 1 percent to 28 percent higher than the number of officially recorded COVID-19 deaths. That is a large spread, so the CDC uses the midpoint, which turns out to be approximately 12 percent.[23]

Another analysis of excess deaths concluded that the U.S. death toll from the virus was probably 36 percent greater than reported.[24] Still another calculation estimates pandemic-related mortality to be 45 percent greater than recorded COVID-19 deaths.[25] On December 29, 2021, The Economist estimated that COVID-19's true worldwide death toll was 18.6 million, more than three times the reported figure.[26] The disparities reflect different criteria for considering deaths to be related to COVID-19. They underscore the challenges of calculating mortality, even in economically advanced countries.

A detailed study that appeared in the British medical journal *The Lancet,* in March 2022, estimated that worldwide excess deaths caused by the pandemic during 2020 and 2021 were more than three times the number of recorded COVID-19 deaths, or 18.2 million instead of the 5.9 million reported at the end of 2021. However, the disparity between excess deaths and recorded COVID-19 deaths varied greatly from region to region and country to country. For the United States, the estimated number of excess deaths was 1.37 times the number of recorded COVID-19 deaths, which is higher than the CDC estimate quoted earlier but closer to the other estimates. *The Lancet* study estimated that excess deaths caused by the pandemic were eight times the recorded COVID deaths in India, twelve times in Egypt, twenty-three times in Pakistan, twenty-six times in Afghanistan, and thirty-three times in Yemen.[27] The study precedes the deaths resulting from the fifth, or Omicron, wave of the pandemic in early 2022.

The death tolls of previous epidemics have also subsequently been revised upward. Initially, the 1918 flu pandemic was estimated to have killed 22 million people. Later research revised the total to 30 million, and it was subsequently raised to between 50 and 100 million.[28] However, later researchers have argued that the Justinian Plague may not have killed as many as were estimated in earlier accounts.[29]

Previous epidemics often raised suspicions that deaths were being deliberately concealed in order to prevent public panic, to protect the economy, or for reasons of political expediency. This was frequently the case during the cholera outbreaks in the nineteenth century. In the fourteenth century and in later waves, the Black Death struck all levels of society—nobles and peasants, rich and poor—although the urban poor were particularly hard-hit. Cholera was seen as a disease of the poor, although wealth brought no guarantee of immunity.

In European cities where the Industrial Revolution had already deepened the chasm between the working classes and the factory owners and merchants who dominated government, cholera sharpened class conflicts. The economic elite tended to see cholera as a disease resulting from the intemperate and dissolute habits of the lower classes. The spread of the disease was blamed on the destitute—for the filthy, crowded conditions in which they lived, for their lack of personal hygiene, for the prevalence of drunkenness and sexual promiscuity. Control of the contagion meant control of the population.

Many in the lower economic ranks of society suspected that cholera was being deliberately spread as part of a diabolical scheme to cull the poor. Some accused the commercial interests of denying, concealing, or dismissing the outbreaks in order to protect commerce or avoid frightening investors—which was, in fact, sometimes the case.

When cholera struck the English port town of Sunderland in 1831, Lord Durham, the most powerful local grandee, and the city's shipping interests were determined to show it as a "wicked falsehood."[30] Likewise, in 1892 the senate of Hamburg delayed the announcement that cholera was present in the city.[31] Italian government officials also conspired to conceal the extent of the cholera outbreak in Naples in 1911.[32]

Early reports of the 1918 flu during the final years of World War I were kept secret by the belligerent powers, fearing that the reports might adversely affect morale or offer enemies an advantage.[33] Spain, which was neutral in World War I, had no such censorship, allowing the Spanish press to report the epidemic first. As a result of it being first reported in Spain, it was called the "Spanish flu." Denials that AIDS was a contagious disease and not the result of poverty and poor nourishment were common. China has been accused of concealing the extent of the COVID-19 outbreak in the city of Wuhan, where the pandemic is believed to have originated.[34]

The United States has its own long history of denials and concealment. When cholera struck New York in 1832, state and local officials refused to take steps to limit the contagion. Instead, they argued that the disease was caused by the immoral lifestyle of the poor, immigrants, and drunks.

As the journalist Sonia Shah has noted, "When a ship carrying cholera-infected passengers arrived in the city's port, officials secretly quarantined the passengers, destroying hospital records to cover it up."[35]

Faced with an outbreak of plague in San Francisco's Chinatown in 1900, the governor of California, worried that it would be bad for business, issued a proclamation denying that there was any plague in "the great and healthful city of San Francisco."[36] He went on to suggest that the health official who discovered the outbreak might have injected the bacilli into the body of a victim *post mortem*. To defend the state's assertions, the governor made it a felony to import plague bacteria, or to make slides or cultures of them, and for newspapers to publish any false report on the presence of bubonic plague. Some in the state legislature thought that the health official responsible for identifying the outbreak should be hanged.

A number of political leaders and online influencers in the United States dismissed the reality of COVID-19, claiming that there was no increase in deaths in 2020 and that the American public had been "gaslighted by the medical industrial complex." The state-level politician responsible for this quote later altered his view, claiming that the virus was "a deadly bio-weapon perpetrated upon the people of the world by enemies foreign, and perhaps domestic."[37]

Some state governments in the United States have been accused of underreporting COVID-19 cases in order to justify reopening their economies after shutdowns or to conceal embarrassing failures of care.[38] Even COVID-19 statistics published by the CDC, long considered the gold standard in epidemiology analysis and reporting, have come under scrutiny.

To match the death toll of the 1918 flu pandemic as a percentage of the world's population—between 2.6 and 5.2 percent—would require more than 200 million COVID-19 deaths, which at present seems highly unlikely. Even that would still be no more than a fraction of the toll of the world's worst epidemics. COVID-19 is not about depopulation leading to a breakdown of society, although such fears drive some responses. Nonetheless, the damage, however it is measured—in financial and economic losses, impact on emotional and psychological health, rending of social fabric, loss of trust, or deepening of political divisions—is significant.

The lower number of deaths from COVID-19 compared

with the numbers from the deadly epidemics of history has allowed greater debate about the danger posed by the present outbreak. While some images from India and South America are deeply disturbing, as well as photos of overwhelmed hospitals in the United States and Europe, we are not seeing bodies piled high in the thousands or mass graves. The numbers being reported in the press are just that—abstract numbers.

In the absence of visible evidence of imminent doom, the risk to human life can be weighed against the risk to economic well-being, individual freedom, or potential social disorder—and people can come to different conclusions. Some have gone so far as to claim that the COVID-19 pandemic is a hoax conjured by government authorities to impose tyrannical controls over the population. This supposed nonexistence is an insidious feature of the current pandemic.

People are resilient and prolific. Wars and epidemics are followed by baby booms. Populations rebound quickly. Church records from sixteenth- and seventeenth-century Europe show dramatic increases in marriages and baptisms in villages devastated by wars or epidemics. Where land was abandoned owing to depopulation, immigrants added to local population growth. Urban populations also grew quickly after epidemics subsided.

Inflows of immigrants were considered essential to economic recovery, and in many cases immigrants were offered incentives to come. To replace the population that had died in the plague, the Italian city-state of Lucca even offered asylum to outlaws from other states. However, the arrival of immigrants also added to social and political tensions.[39]

The COVID-19 pandemic has not caused depopulation, so the current circumstances are very different. Although Europe faces declining populations owing to lower birth rates and emigration from poorer European countries, immigrants and refugees from outside Europe have not been universally welcomed and their presence has already increased social tensions. Arrivals of large numbers of immigrants, especially from the Middle East and Africa, where already weak economies will recover from the pandemic more slowly, will further aggravate the situation.

There is little debate that the COVID-19 pandemic has already had far-reaching consequences, especially damage to global and local economies and to the welfare of millions of individuals. Although some nations will bounce back quickly, assuming the pandemic fades in 2022, it will likely take years for the world to fully recover. And some economic scarring will be deep and permanent. The economic consequences of the current pandemic are the subject of the next chapter.

CHAPTER 2:
DEEP ECONOMIC SCARS

THOUGH IT IS still not fully calculated—and perhaps it will never be accurately known—the impact of the COVID-19 pandemic on the global economy has been disastrous. According to the U.S. Congressional Research Service, the pandemic has negatively affected global economic growth "beyond anything experienced in nearly a century."[1] The World Bank said it has produced the deepest global recession since World War II, more than twice as deep as the recession associated with the 2007–2008 financial crisis. The U.S. GDP plunged at an annual rate of 31.4 percent in the second quarter of 2020.[2] The largest fraction of economies saw the largest declines in per capita output since 1870.[3] This was the widest contraction since the beginning of the Great Depression.

The technical jargon and statistics assembled by economists and financial institutions do not convey the human toll. The deep economic recession caused by COVID-19 affects people's lives in a variety of ways, though not uniformly in America or around the world. The most obvious impact is unemployment. In 2020, the global rate of unemployment reached its highest level since 1965.[4]

It recovered some in 2021 and was projected to improve further in 2022, but will still remain higher than it was just prior to the pandemic.[5] (This projection preceded the devastating summer Delta and Omicron surges.[6])

In the United States, unemployment levels jumped significantly at the beginning of the pandemic, with the U.S. rate reaching 14.8 percent in April 2020.[7] But, despite the continuing pandemic, jobs returned and employment recovered with the unemployment rate dropping to 3.6 percent by March 2022, only slightly above where it was in December 2019, at the beginning of the pandemic.

On average, people in the United States were making more money at the end of 2021 than they did a year earlier. But "on average" does not reflect the disparities. According to a report by the British charity Oxfam, the ten richest men in the world doubled their wealth during the COVID-19 pandemic, while 160 million other people are projected to have been pushed into poverty.[8] The methodology used by Oxfam has come under challenge, but there are other indisputable indicators of disparity. People with money in the stock market did extremely well during the pandemic's first two years. The U.S. Standard & Poor's 500 stock index rose 16.3 percent in 2020 and 26.9 percent in 2021, closing the year at virtually an all-time high.

And while it is true that most workers in the United States, as of late 2021, were earning higher wages than before the pandemic, people with higher education and professional skills fared better, as most of the salary increases benefited the skilled/professional classes. In contrast, people living paycheck-to-paycheck, with fewer skills and less education—and usually without retirement plans—were severely impacted. A report by the Board of Governors of the Federal Reserve System examining the beginning of the pandemic states: "In the United States, vulnerable populations, such as low- and moderate-income communities and racial and ethnic minorities, have been particularly hard hit."[9]

The COVID-19 pandemic financially affected young and lower-skilled workers more severely than workers with skills and jobs that enabled them to continue to work from home.[10] Women suffered more than men.[11] Women in the labor force depend heavily on child care or children being in schools. When schools and childcare facilities close down, women are more likely to be forced to give up their jobs or to be prevented from going back to work.

Workers in many developed countries also received supplementary government payments during the pandemic, which particularly benefited low and moderate earners. Governments also imposed temporary moratoriums on residential evictions and provided other forms of protection. As these supplementary benefits end or are curtailed, and the support they have provided is exhausted, the impact of the pandemic on ordinary workers could increase.

And even as jobs are coming back in some places, since the pandemic is accelerating preexisting trends toward automation and digitalization, many of the jobs lost are never coming back. In some industries, companies may conclude that they no longer need to provide the same level of service they provided before the pandemic.[12] Many workers will have to change what they do or where they work—and maybe both. Displacement often means smaller paychecks. Living standards, on average, have declined, especially with the decline of manufacturing-sector jobs and the increase of service-sector jobs.

Pandemics affect the world unevenly. Times are harder in some countries than in others and they are harder for some people than others. What economists call "emerging markets" and "low-income countries" have suffered significantly more than countries with advanced economies and their recovery will likely be slower.[13]

The Black Death, which caused enormous loss of life, in the long run actually improved the situation of those lower on the economic scale. Depopulation made labor scarce, enabling surviving workers to command higher wages. Cultivated land was abandoned, and rents became cheaper. With fewer mouths to feed, the price of food fell. The vast economic chasm between lords and peasants was, for a while, reduced.[14] The Justinian Plague caused a sufficient number of deaths to produce a similar effect.

The more recent epidemics experienced by the world have not resulted in depopulation; they have disrupted economies and societies. Workers remain in ample supply, while jobs are lost. Instead of reducing the distance between the rich and the poor—already viewed as a problem before 2020—the COVID-19 pandemic will exacerbate existing inequality.

The post–World War II pandemics—the Hong Kong flu in 1968, the HIV/AIDS pandemic that began in the 1980s, SARS (severe acute respiratory syndrome) in 2003, the swine flu in 2009, MERS (Middle East Respiratory Syndrome) in 2012, the 2014–2016 Ebola epidemic, and the 2016 Zika virus epidemic—caused parallel economic damage in the areas they affected. Ebola had a severe effect on parts of Africa, and Zika impacted Latin America, but in the United States and Europe these epidemics had little effect beyond producing fear. SARS had a large impact on Asia but not on the United States. The impact of MERS on the United States was probably even smaller.

Given the scale of the COVID-19 pandemic and the fact that it has spread throughout the world, the economic damage caused by it will be deeper and longer.[15] Emerging economies and less-developed countries will suffer disproportionately. The COVID-19 pandemic will likely push hundreds of millions of people into absolute poverty.[16] Whereas relative poverty means having less than an average income—enough for the basics but little else—absolute, or extreme, poverty means not having enough money for the basics: food, shelter, clothing. For the past thirty years, economic progress has steadily reduced the number of people living in absolute poverty. The COVID-19 pandemic has now reversed that trend, and it may take years to turn it around again.

The pandemic has affected countries and people unequally, and the recovery will also be uneven. Some countries are snapping back from COVID-19 faster than expected. The world's economic superpowers appear to be shrugging off its effects and rapidly recovering, although the emergence of the more contagious Omicron variant in November 2021 complicated the recovery. China quickly bounced back, but then was severely affected by the new wave of the virus in the spring of 2022 and forced to impose strict controls that curtailed commercial activity. The United States also made a comparatively rapid comeback. Europe and Japan appear to be recovering more slowly.[17] Meanwhile, less-developed countries may fall further behind.

Even in the economically most advanced countries of the world, public health systems have struggled to cope with the casualties of the contagion, especially the more contagious Omicron variant. Countries with less-robust health-care systems are overwhelmed. Vaccines are slower to arrive in poorer nations.[18] A November 2021 report by the Economist Intelligence Unit noted the unequal distribution of COVID vaccines and uneven vaccination rates even where they are available.[19] As some European countries pushed the percentage of their populations fully vaccinated into the 90s,[20] many African countries in the final months of 2021 were still around the 1 percent mark.

As of late 2021, the United States, Canada, Chile, Argentina, Brazil, and Cuba, most of Europe, Morocco, Saudi Arabia, China, Mongolia, Japan, Singapore, Australia, and New Zealand have vaccinated the majority of their populations. If present trends continue, Egypt, the Balkans, Russia, Central Asia, and India will have done so by late 2022. However, the populations of Bolivia, most of Central America, most of Africa, and much of the Middle East, along with Pakistan, Bangladesh, Myanmar, Papua New Guinea, and North Korea, are not likely to be widely vaccinated before 2023 or later.[21] And this projection assumes that there will not be a new mutant strain that is impervious to the current vaccines.

Africa—where, as of late 2021, less than 6 percent of the population had been vaccinated and, in many of the African countries, only around 1 percent had been vaccinated—is especially vulnerable. By March 2022, this situation had improved, but still, fewer than 20 percent of the population in most countries in Africa had received a single dose, and in fifteen African nations fewer than 10 percent were fully vaccinated.[22] The continent already faces a financial crisis that is likely to be worsened by inflation, along with potential food shortages resulting from the war in Ukraine. In addition, a number of African countries are engulfed in armed conflicts that impede health care and economic progress. Economic collapse in Africa—a volatile region that is the source of continued migration pressure on Europe—can be averted only by accelerating vaccination and continuing generous foreign assistance.[23]

Thus far, Africa has not recorded the large numbers of cases and deaths seen in Europe and the United States. Scientists are uncertain as to why. Some believe it may reflect the more rural nature of Africa's population—although Lagos in Nigeria has more than 20 million inhabitants and Kinshasa in the Democratic Republic of the Congo has nearly 15 million. The comparative youth of Africa's population may be another factor. Others speculate that exposure to other diseases such as malaria may provide some as-yet-unidentified protection.[24] Part of the explanation could simply be undercounting. *The Lancet* study of excess deaths mentioned earlier estimated that while excess deaths resulting from COVID-19 worldwide were three times greater than recorded figures, excess deaths in sub-Saharan Africa were estimated to be fourteen times greater. That would put the mortality rate in Africa closer to the world figure.[25]

The direct and indirect health consequences of a continuing pandemic on vulnerable populations—delayed medical treatment, other health conditions ignored—will last longer than the economic effects, further delaying people's ability to recover economically. The governments of poorer countries have less money to restore public health systems, mitigate economic damage, or kick-start their economies.

Deterioration of skills during periods of unemployment, long lapses in the use and maintenance of machinery during shutdowns, and failure to replace equipment will reduce efficiency and productivity. Business closures result in loss of contacts and erosion of business networks and lead to permanent loss of experience and knowledge—valuable commodities in all economies but even more precious in less-developed economies. Education losses have also been more severe in low-income developing countries.[26] Remote learning has proved difficult even in advanced countries, where computers are more abundant and Internet access is available. Unequal access to computers and the Internet has been a problem in the United States; the issue was much worse in less-developed countries.

Some forms of foreign aid may decline as wealthier nations are obliged to deal with their own problems. The current pandemic and its associated shutdowns have put many governments in difficult economic straits as they attempt to mitigate the economic effects on their own populations. Tax revenues have declined with the contraction in economic activity. Government deficits have grown. Vaccinating the population, restoring the economy, and improving public health at home will take priority over foreign aid. Foreign-assistance budgets will be especially vulnerable to cuts.

Foreign investment may also weaken as corporations face uncertainties about the landscape of the post-pandemic world. Confrontations between great powers, economic sanctions, and tariff wars—issues that predated the pandemic—will complicate decisions. With political protests continuing around the world, civil unrest is now seen as a leading source of global business risk.[27]

WILL COVID-19 PROMOTE DEGLOBALIZATION?

Prior to the pandemic, globalization and free trade were articles of faith for many economists. In China alone, globalization and free trade brought hundreds of millions of people out of poverty. Manufacturing became an increasingly global and increasingly complex enterprise with raw materials and component parts moving across the planet to final assembly points and customers worldwide. To reduce the costs of building huge factories and holding large inventories, companies adopted "just-in-time" manufacturing processes, where materials and parts would be timed to arrive precisely at the moment they were needed. Everything depended on exquisitely coordinated logistics. But while just-in-time manufacturing increased efficiency and reduced costs, it also increased vulnerabilities to disruption. A traffic jam at the Canadian border could shut down automobile assembly lines in the United States. A single iPhone contains components from suppliers in forty-three countries.

The COVID-19 pandemic has upended supply chains. It may contribute to further deglobalization as countries and corporations seek to reduce their vulnerability to disruptions that come with dependence on complex global supply chains.[28] That may be good news for workers who have lost jobs to outsourcing, but it is bad news for workers in countries that are dependent on being part of a global economy. Generally, a reduction in international trade adversely affects total economic output—everybody's economy. It could also increase the price of goods now made in other countries and accelerate investments in automation, reducing jobs everywhere. Interestingly, this simultaneously creates inflationary pressures from price increases and deflationary pressures from automation.

The COVID-19 pandemic has caused huge bottlenecks in international shipping, with cascading impacts on manufacturing and trade, ultimately contributing to inflationary pressures. In the early 2000s, I was consulting with a major multinational corporation on crisis management issues. Mindful of the disruptive effects on the economy of the 9/11 attacks, the challenge to the corporate risk team was to identify events that could cause major economic damage—losses of a billion dollars or more—to the corporation.

We looked at political risks, such as wars, that could disrupt offshore manufacturing and just-in-time global supply chains. We also examined a number of scenarios involving cyberattacks (this was years before the recent ransomware attacks). We thought about natural disasters. We ultimately reached the conclusion that there were relatively few events capable of causing damage on that scale.

One such event was a worldwide pandemic, which was very much on our minds given the 2003 outbreak of SARS that affected Asia, where much of the corporation's manufacturing took place. (In October 2021, Apple announced that pandemic-related supply disruptions had cost it $6 billion in its fiscal fourth quarter.[29]) One question for us, then, was how the corporation might mitigate economic damage if China was unable to produce and export.

Using the 1918 flu, the 1957 Asian flu, and the 1968 Hong Kong flu pandemics as templates, we were able to graphically display the spread, trajectory, and duration of a hypothetical pandemic and explore preparatory and response strategies. How long would it take the company to set up new manufacturing lines in other countries? How much might a pandemic depress demand? Should (and could) the company evacuate expatriate employees?

The theoretical model suggested that the time required to set up new assembly lines could mean that they would come into production just as the pandemic was subsiding. The company could have backup facilities ready, but that was a costly undertaking, and the skills to run such facilities were not locally available. We also realized that arranging transfers and work visas and moving people during a pandemic would be difficult.

Of course, we were mindful that the 1918 flu pandemic and others before it came in waves, but the waves affected the world unevenly. The corporation would have to correctly guess the timing and geography of each next wave. Exposure to international disruptions could be reduced by bringing its manufacturing back home, but, just as its sourcing was global, its products were sold worldwide. "Re-shoring" could reduce, but not eliminate, exposure.

One possible solution was to have an early warning system that, upon the outbreak of any contagious disease, would activate a special crisis management team to monitor the progress of the disease, identify mitigating measures, and inform management of necessary decisions. Another possible approach was to temporarily abandon just-in-time deliveries and push shipping of vital components forward at the first indication of possible supply chain disruptions. This, too, was complicated.

Looking back after experiencing the COVID-19 pandemic, it is clear that the company's early planning effort, while useful, did not identify all of the complexities of a major worldwide pandemic. As a consequence of COVID-19, many corporations with international operations are probably going through similar exercises now. Indeed, until the pandemic, many smaller companies may not even have realized the extent to which they had international exposure, some of which may have been indirect.

Re-shoring is easier said than done, even for simple items. For some corporations, reducing dependence on offshore manufacturing of critical components might be a realistic strategy—some degree of deglobalization can be anticipated, but these decisions are complex. The problem is that the supply chain has evolved over the years, with most firms adopting a just-in-time inventory strategy. There is not much wiggle room. The practice of offshoring made products cheaper to buy but, at the same time, decimated American manufacturing and made companies more vulnerable to disruptions.

By 2019, the United States relied so heavily on China for personal protective equipment that domestic production could not be ramped up fast enough to meet needs. For significantly more complex manufactured items, the difficulty is even greater. In the case of computer chips, for example, it can take years to build a chip foundry and establish its needed network of suppliers. Even if the United States decided to produce chips at home, it would still be years away from producing the sophisticated chips that one company in Taiwan currently makes. The COVID-19 vaccines themselves required inputs from a number of countries in an incredibly complex production process.

In addition, the problems of re-shoring are not simply a matter of parts. Even though factory floors are now highly automated, the United States does not have enough skilled workers. Companies will not make the necessary investment in production facilities and training if they feel that the issue is a short-term challenge, but the cost-benefit calculus will most likely be different in the case of the COVID-19 pandemic. Is the pandemic a once-in-a-century event or a chronic condition that will persist? The war in Ukraine and the economic sanctions will complicate calculations.

Jobs in developing and less-developed economies will be slow to return. Re-shoring will further cut down on recovery in those economies. Countries where local economies and employment depend on services, foreign employment, or tourism will have the toughest comeback. Airline travel and international tourism, which account for an important share of the global economy, have been shattered.[30] Numerous large corporations—restaurant chains, department stores, car rental companies—have gone bankrupt. Many small businesses have closed forever. Unemployment will remain high in some countries for years to come. Remittances—a lifeline for families in developing countries—are likely to decline.

In March 2022, the U.S. unemployment rate fell to 3.6 percent, which is low by historical standards. However, that low rate does not reveal the full picture. In some parts of the country, the unemployment rate remains nearly 7 percent. Nor does the national figure reflect the fact that the number of long-term unemployed (those jobless for twenty-seven weeks or more), which doubled at the beginning of the pandemic in February 2020 to 2.2 million workers, had dropped only to 1.4 million workers by March 2022—leaving it still more than 300,000 higher than at the beginning of the pandemic. The long-term unemployed comprise 23.9 percent of all unemployed persons. In addition to these numbers are the 5.7 million people who want to work but who are no longer actively looking for a job (and thus are not considered unemployed in many U.S. statistics). The number of people not in the labor force who want a job is always a challenging category to reduce, but its number as of March 2022 remains 700,000 higher than it was at the beginning of the pandemic.[31]

AMERICA'S "GREAT RESIGNATION"

The improved situation of the peasants following the Black Death reflected the large-scale depopulation that resulted from the plague. The 1918 flu pandemic had a far lower mortality rate but was also accompanied and followed by a burst of labor militancy. In 1919, coal miners, steelworkers, railroad men, dressmakers, and others in the United States demanded shorter hours and higher wages. Safer work conditions and ending child labor and the exploitation of women workers were also issues.

In part, the increased militancy reflected the power that workers had gained as a consequence of World War

I. Wages went up during the war, although strikes were prohibited in many countries during the war years for national security reasons. The Russian Revolution in 1917 may also have been a source of inspiration. The 1918 flu, which was particularly deadly to young adults, may have played a contributing role.[32] The effects of a pandemic, however, ought not to be judged solely in terms of economic leverage, but in psychological terms as well. As we'll discuss later, epidemics expose inequalities in society. The poor had suffered badly from the 1918 flu, and this made colonial subjects acutely aware of the inequalities in how their imperial rulers responded to the disease. The prospect of death also promotes reassessments of one's own personal circumstances. A million reassessments can produce a mass movement.

It is noteworthy that while the COVID-19 pandemic has contributed to unemployment and economic hardship, especially in developing countries, it has in a number of economically advanced countries led to wildcat strikes and manifestations of increased worker independence. The United States saw a resurgence of labor activism and work stoppages during the pandemic, although labor strikes remained well below historical levels.

Most of the strikes involved workers who felt that their health and safety were being endangered by the pandemic and that their employers were not doing enough to protect them or compensate them adequately for the risk.[33] Many of the strikers worked in high-exposure jobs—in fast food outlets or other retail businesses, as delivery personnel or bus drivers, in crowded assembly or food processing lines, as health workers. Many of these workers already had limited access to health care. Reflecting the long decline in private-sector labor unions, most of the strikes were local affairs rather than industrywide shutdowns.

Labor activism was further fueled by the fact that American corporations in 2021 recorded their highest profit margins since 1950.[34] Major corporations have continued to vigorously oppose unions throughout the pandemic. Under public pressure, politicians have passed relief packages to help companies and to protect jobs and mitigate lost incomes. The packages included eviction moratoriums and debt holidays in economically developed countries. But many politicians remained unsympathetic, arguing that those who left jobs should not be eligible for unemployment benefits, or that generous government handouts had removed the incentive to work—and that benefits should therefore be cut to force people back to work.

In fact, individual Americans got about one-fifth of the $4 trillion in economic relief grants, loans, and tax breaks spent by the government to keep the American economy going during the pandemic, while $2.3 trillion went to businesses whether or not they were affected by the pandemic or kept workers on their payroll during shutdowns.[35]

The principal point here goes beyond labor unions, corporate profits, and public funding—those are always topics of intense debate in democratic and capitalist societies. It is a matter of whether people already suffering protracted stress, like that caused by the pandemic, see the response as fair. Widespread economic disruption, coupled with perceptions of unequal suffering, heightened inequality, greed, and corruption, cause deep resentments that play out in unpredictable ways.

The temporary easing of the pandemic and of government-imposed shutdowns produced another phenomenon: many workers refused to return to on-site jobs, citing health concerns. By June 2021, the number of American workers voluntarily leaving their jobs rose by 164,000, to 942,000.[36] That number rose to 4.4 million in September 2021, surpassing in a single month the total of 4 million workers who walked off their jobs in 1919.[37] Europe witnessed a similar phenomenon, although not at the levels seen in the United States.[38]

The COVID-19 pandemic has no doubt caused many to review their life situations—widespread death has that effect. However, the majority of those leaving their jobs are not leaving the workforce to contemplate forest ponds or write poetry. They are moving to the better-paying jobs that are on offer, which suggests that their motivations are pragmatic. The highest percentage of those leaving their jobs are those with high school diplomas or less, which usually means that they are leaving minimum-wage jobs and poorer working conditions.[39] Although the United States has the world's largest economy, according to statistics compiled by the Organisation for Economic Co-operation and Development (OECD), the United States also has the highest percentage of low-wage earners of all the economically advanced countries.[40]

Companies large and small are also having difficulty recruiting employees. Vacancies have remained high. Pay is an issue. Adjusting for inflation, American workers on average earn less today than they did in 1968 and have fewer benefits. But it is not just a matter of more pay. Worker demands also involve working conditions, flexible hours, a better work-life balance. The phenomenon may also reflect a new sense of leverage, not unlike that of Europe's peasants in the fourteenth century. However, these phenomena may only be temporary as recent figures indicate that participation in the labor force increased and as of early 2022 was only slightly below its level on the eve on the pandemic. At the same time, self-employment increased by 600,000. This category includes "gig workers" who are actually employees of companies, but classified as independent contractors. But it also includes people starting their own businesses.[41]

AN UNCERTAIN TRAJECTORY

While initial statistics show economically advanced countries recovering in spite of supply chain difficulties, uncertainty prevails as the pandemic continues and new variants wash across the planet. In a World Economic Forum report released in January 2022, global economic experts believed that the global recovery will be volatile and uneven over the next three years (2022–2024). Only one in six of those surveyed were optimistic. An uneven global recovery from the pandemic was "among the four top risks identified by experts, along with climate failure, growing social divides [heightened by the pandemic] and heightened cyber risks."[42] Among the top ten short-term risks identified were extreme weather events, livelihood crises, social cohesion erosion, infectious diseases, and mental health deterioration—the latter primarily consequences of the pandemic. Social cohesion erosion and involuntary migration were among the top ten long-term risks.

We do not know how this ends. The post-pandemic economic landscape is still unclear. National self-reliance is desirable in a pandemic but, as we have already seen, it can easily turn into hoarding of medical equipment and vaccines, and it can promote more virulent forms of economic nationalism. Will the post-pandemic economy be less globalized, and does that mean it will be poorer? Will it be even more unequal?

Can we even talk about a *post-pandemic* economy? Or will the future be a continuing pandemic, with surges in various regions of the world or recurring, worldwide bouts reflecting new mutations? That would cause periodic shutdowns, requiring permanent increases in healthcare investments and periodic economic relief packages. It would mean continuing economic uncertainty, limiting investment. It could reverse globalization, reduce trade, and create permanent barriers to travel and immigration, and it could have long-term effects on international tourism.

CHAPTER 3:
EFFECTS ON SOCIETY

IN HIS 1919 book *The Autumn of the Middle Ages*, Dutch cultural historian Johan Huizinga described European society after the fourteenth-century plague as highly strung, on edge, quick to violence.[1] "So fierce and clamorous was life," he wrote, "that it could endure the mingled odor of blood and roses."[2] Could this also turn out to be a description of society, especially American society, after the COVID-19 pandemic?

While the death toll and economic destruction of a pandemic are easier to quantify, the effects of the COVID-19 pandemic on society are significant but insidious. Some manifestations are readily observable, but how long these will last and how they may affect future behavior are less certain. Further insights into the possibilities can be gained by considering the societal effects of past pandemics, where we have the benefit of a long-term perspective.

Historians of past epidemics would not be surprised by the defiance of government-ordered measures to slow the spread of COVID-19. Since the Middle Ages, it has been recognized that large-scale outbreaks of disease are dangerous and demand aggressive responses, drawing government into domains of activity that have traditionally been outside of political authority. Physical separation—keeping the disease away—has been the principal strategy, especially when there was little understanding of how contagions spread and no effective medical treatment for those who contracted the disease.

The Bible was one source of medical strategy in Western society. Plague victims were treated as lepers—outcasts who could have no contact with people who were not afflicted. During the Black Death, houses where people were affected were marked with a red cross, and no one could enter or leave. The dead were put out into the street at night to be taken to plague pits. Walled cities closed their gates. Affected towns and neighborhoods were sealed off and, in some cases, were abandoned or destroyed. Travel and trade were restricted. People who were possibly exposed were quarantined—kept apart until they presented no danger. The visibly ill were removed and taken to special hospitals, segregation camps, or pesthouses, often to die. Loved ones were unceremoniously buried in mass graves.

Those quarantined were kept on board remotely moored ships, put on isolated islands, or housed in huts away from the rest of the population. The wealthy could remove themselves to distant residences; the poor had no such option. In response to continuing waves of the plague, some

European cities built huge lazarettos—the term comes from the Italian word for *beggar*—part-hospital, part-prison, where diseased poor persons were held until they died or survived the illness. Survivors were sent to clean the houses of others affected by the contagion or to perform other necessary functions for the city.

Not knowing what caused the diseases, some governments tried to also impose dietary restrictions, for example, prohibiting the consumption of alcohol or unripe or overripe fruit. These restrictions were widely ignored and, in some cases, openly mocked.[3] Understanding of the way pathogens spread brought new measures: social distancing, face masks, mandatory shutdowns, curfews, vaccination.

As Frank Snowden noted in *Epidemics and Society*, these efforts, while understandable from a public health perspective, marked "a significant extension of state power into spheres of human life that had never before been subject to political authority."[4] But as Snowden points out, these measures "justified control over the economy and the movement of people; they authorized surveillance and forcible detention; and they sanctioned the invasion of homes and the extinction of civil liberties [or what people saw as their 'rights' at various times in history]."[5] Not surprisingly, they provoked resistance.

The nineteenth-century cholera outbreaks in Europe occurred during a period when the conservative wealthy saw the urban masses as reservoirs of disease and discontent to be quarantined and controlled. Authorities imposed *cordons sanitaires*—guarded lines preventing people and goods from an area known to be infected by a disease from entering areas where the disease had not been detected. *Cordons sanitaires* proliferated in Europe in the nineteenth century and were increasingly enforced by armies. In 1821, for example, France deployed troops on its border with Spain to prevent the spread of a yellow fever epidemic then raging in Barcelona.[6]

The militarization of *cordons sanitaires* reflected a more authoritarian approach to combating contagious disease. This expansion of state authority coincided with the tendency, especially among conservatives, to conflate poverty, disease, and political disorder. To prevent the spread of disease required enforcing obedience among people who were despised because of their class and assumed dissolute lifestyle, but were also considered dangerous to the social order. Suppression in both the health and political sense required a hard response.

In the nineteenth century, before the development of modern civilian police departments, military and auxiliary units (the Yeomanry Cavalry in Britain and the Cossacks in Russia) were regularly deployed to disperse political demonstrators, break up strikes, and deal with cholera riots. While the sources of unrest differed, their suppression engaged the same state actors.

The imposition of *cordons sanitaires* as a public health measure declined during the twentieth century, and the term was increasingly used in the purely political sense to denote a barrier to the spread of dangerous ideologies, which came to be seen in the same terms as contagious diseases.

In America, the response to contagious disease was historically also one of enforcement, which on occasion brought a militarized response. The Commissioned Corps of the U.S. Public Health Service, which traces its origins back to 1798, is a uniformed service of commissioned officers commanded by the Surgeon General. One of its original missions was the enforcement of quarantines. From the beginning of the Republic into the twentieth century, quarantines were imposed to control smallpox, typhoid, cholera, plague, yellow fever, diphtheria, and other diseases.[7]

As in Europe, there was resistance in the United States to health mandates. Enforcement sometimes reflected racial attitudes, notably in the 1899 plague outbreak in Honolulu and the 1900–1908 plague epidemic in San Francisco. In both cases, the cities' Chinatowns were the epicenters of the plague.

Many in the non-Chinese community mistakenly believed that the disease infected only the Chinese, who lived in crowded and filthy conditions, and that whites were immune. Contagion control measures and anti-Chinese sentiments combined to produce clumsy enforcement.

During a plague outbreak in 1899, a fire set by the authorities to destroy a plague-infested building in Honolulu's Chinatown swept out of control, burning down the entire neighborhood and displacing thousands of residents. This was the second time Honolulu's Chinatown had burned. In November 1885, anti-Chinese rioters had driven the Chinese out and burned down the area. Two days later, anti-Chinese rioters drove the Chinese out and burned down Tacoma, Washington's Chinatown. Targets of continuing prejudice, facing economic ruin, and steeped in their own cultural beliefs, the Chinese remained understandably suspicious of the authorities and health workers.

Then, as now, defiance of measures implemented to prevent the spread of a disease and protect populations led to civil disobedience and social unrest. Restrictions on movement and commerce threatened livelihoods. Isolation impeded social contact and increased individual anxieties.

During cholera outbreaks in the nineteenth century, residents flouted municipal regulations banning public assemblies. Quarantines and restrictions on commerce provoked protests, which sometimes turned violent. Political leaders and health officials were vilified and, in some cases, physically attacked. During the 1884 cholera epidemic in Naples, Snowden notes, "on some occasions, unwanted medical interventions ignited full-scale rebellions."[8]

Suspicion of government is a recurring theme. There were suspicions that ulterior political motives drove assertions of authority based on health crises. The broad powers granted to enforcers of draconian measures in the Middle Ages opened opportunities for extortion. Similar allegations against the police arose in India during the response to the third plague in the 1890s.[9] Extortion is something we have not heard much about in current circumstances, although allegations of favoritism and corruption have arisen in connection with the vaccination program.

As in past epidemics, suspicions that government has exploited COVID-19 to expand its authority have been widespread. One commentator warned that lockdowns, "under the guise of a real medical pandemic," were turning the United States into "a totalitarian state."[10]

Resistance to wearing masks is not new. Sixteenth-century plague doctors, particularly in Venice, wore elaborate personal protective equipment. They covered their faces with odd masks that had glass eyes and long beaks, which were filled with lavender, herbs, and spices to protect the wearer from the dangerous fumes believed to carry the plague. The doctors wore thick coats, boots, and gloves to protect their skin from contact, and they carried canes to permit them to examine patients without directly touching them. By the eighteenth century, the elaborate costumes had fallen out of use.

The requirement for medical workers, police, and ordinary citizens to wear masks began during the 1918 flu pandemic. Americans were urged to wear masks, and in some cities authorities made wearing masks mandatory for police forces, medical workers, and even ordinary citizens. Masks came in many styles and probably did not meet the standards required to protect wearers against the virus—although widespread mask-wearing in San Francisco may have been partially responsible for limiting the number of deaths.[11]

Inspired by the patriotism that accompanied World War I, many wore masks as a demonstration that they were doing their part. But then, as now, not everyone accepted the requirement. Those who failed to wear their masks were arrested and fined; courts in San Francisco were reportedly overloaded with mask violators.[12]

Mandatory mask-wearing has provoked outrage in both the United States and Europe during the COVID-19 pandemic. Opponents in the United Kingdom have called mandatory mask-wearing a "monstrous imposition" that threatens fundamental liberties.[13] In America's deeply divided society, attitudes toward masks have, like everything else, reflected political views and party affiliations. According to a poll in 2020, 49 percent of Democrats said they always wore a protective face mask when outside their homes, compared with 26 percent of Republicans; 46 percent of Republicans said they never wore a mask, compared with 18 percent of Democrats. Mask wearers had greater trust in scientists.[14] Those who resisted mask-wearing trusted leaders who scoffed at the reality of the virus or downplayed its seriousness and disparaged health officials for overreacting. These differences have led to angry confrontations and even physical violence in places of business, on public transportation, and in other public spheres where masks have been required.

As the pandemic continued, public support for mask and vaccine mandates increased in the United States, although attitudes continued to reflect political allegiances. According to an August 17–18, 2021, poll, an overwhelming 72 percent versus 28 percent of Americans favored mask mandates as a "matter of health and safety," and did not consider them an infringement on personal liberty. By 61 to 39 percent, they endorsed requiring vaccinations except for those with medical or religious exemptions.[15]

The history of resistance to vaccination goes back at least 250 years, to the 1770s. The Chinese had reportedly developed a means of inoculating against smallpox as early as 200 B.C.E.—grinding the scabs from those infected into a powder and inhaling it.[16] The technique eventually spread to Europe and America. Benjamin Franklin, who lost a son to smallpox in 1759, wrote a preface to a report that year arguing for the effectiveness of inoculation. In it, he noted that the practice divided the people, with some accepting it and others rejecting it. The latter group, Franklin noted, suspected that doctors magnified the number of people killed by smallpox while concealing the number who died as a result of inoculation.[17]

By the middle of the nineteenth century, a safer vaccine based on cowpox and vaccinia was routinely being used to prevent smallpox. Vaccinating infants became mandatory in the United Kingdom in 1853, but the law provoked immediate resistance, leading to violent riots in several cities and prompting the organization of the Anti-Vaccination League in London.[18]

Resistance to vaccination was especially pronounced in the United States. The Anti-Vaccination Society of America was founded in 1879.[19] Mandatory vaccination against smallpox was not ordered and upheld by the U.S. Supreme Court until 1905, with individual states allowing for religious and philosophical exemptions.[20] The society argued against compulsory vaccination on grounds that it represented the introduction of foreign substances into the body, that medical professionals' claims that it was effective were suspect, and that it was a violation of the First Amendment guarantee of religious freedom.

The rapid creation of a vaccine to prevent infection or ameliorate the effects of COVID-19, along with government-led efforts to vaccinate the population, provoked similar resistance. Anti-vaxxers claimed that the vaccine was ineffective, with some asserting that it was a plot to implant microchips for the purpose of later surveillance and control.[21] American anti-vaxxers joined with libertarians to raise the same First Amendment arguments that had been raised earlier. What distinguishes the current anti-vaccination movement is its close correlation with political party affiliation, with acceptance of vaccines strongest among Democrats and resistance strongest among Republicans. This, in turn, results in a clear geographic divide and suggests that future vaccination efforts will also break along political lines.

INEQUALITY BARED

Like the COVID-19 pandemic, previous epidemics also frayed the fabric of society. "Every man for himself" attitudes prevailed. Those who could do so fled for their lives, abandoning more-vulnerable relatives. Hoarding led to artificial shortages and fights. According to the fourteenth century Italian poet Giovanni Boccaccio, people in Florence behaved like animals during the plague. The poor fared especially badly. With no one to care for them, many ended their lives in the streets.[22] Concern for both the living and the dead declined. Family members were abandoned. "Doctors, druggists, and the surveying purveyors of food charged exorbitant prices for provisions and services to the sick."[23] Today, the hoarding of oxygen tanks by wealthy families has hampered India's ability to treat coronavirus patients. The United States has seen fistfights over hand sanitizer, toilet paper, and paper towels at big box stores. Angry altercations have occurred at upscale supermarkets.

Epidemics affect economic classes unequally. When the Black Death struck Florence in the fourteenth century, wealthier citizens could flee to their country villas. It is no different today. Escape is an option for today's mobile elite, who can retreat to ranches in Wyoming or villages in the south of France. A larger number can reduce risk by working from home and doing their shopping online. These solutions are less available to those—often the lowest-paid workers—with jobs that require their presence. Again, perceptions of unfairness contribute to long-term resentments.

In the United States, socioeconomic status often reflects race or ethnicity. According to the CDC, Black or African Americans are 1.1 times more likely than white, non-Hispanic persons to contract COVID-19, and 1.9

times more likely to die. Hispanics or Latinos are 2 times more likely to get COVID-19 and 2.3 times more likely to die. Native Americans are 1.6 times more likely to get COVID-19 and 2.4 times more likely to die. Rates for Asian Americans closely match those of the white, non-Hispanic population.[24]

A study of the socioeconomic determinants of COVID-19 infections in England and Wales showed that areas with larger households, low levels of self-reported health, and a larger proportion of people using public transport (seen as indicators of lower-income communities) have higher infection rates.[25] Black Brazilians are more likely to die from COVID-19 than white Brazilians.[26] The pandemic has deepened caste inequality in India.[27] These divergences reflect overlapping race, caste, and class issues. COVID-19 will leave a legacy of lasting resentments.

BLAMING OTHERS

History's epidemics do not create popular prejudices; they reinforce existing ones by creating opportunities for racist rabble-rousers and populist politicians. Nationalist and nativist tendencies intensify. Outsiders become sources of suspicion. To assuage public wrath and deflect blame for their own helplessness or incompetence, political leaders faced with the consequences of public health crises may endorse, even encourage, allegations that the epidemic is someone else's fault.

Athenians blamed the plague that devastated their city in the fifth century B.C.E. on their Spartan enemies, who, it was rumored, had poisoned Athens's reservoirs. (When a plague struck Sparta centuries later, its then-Christian ruler expelled the city's entire Jewish population.) Romans faced with the Antonine Plague blamed Christians, whom they regarded as a dangerous religious sect. The people of Byzantium blamed the Justinian Plague on the licentious behavior of Empress Theodora, whom many already despised.

Many blame China for the spread of the COVID-19 pandemic, but in the fourth century, when an epidemic (likely smallpox) spread through Chinese forces fighting against nomadic tribes on the northern frontier, the Chinese blamed the outbreak on their adversaries, calling it the "barbarian pox" or "captive's pox" because it was brought into China by prisoners captured by the Chinese.[28] The Black Death of the fourteenth century is also believed to have originated in the steppes of Central Asia.

Throughout history, Jews have been targets of popular anger. Accused of poisoning wells to cause the Black Death, thousands of Jews were massacred across Europe. Large groups were rounded up and pushed into pits, where they were burned alive. Local authorities were present at these mass murders, indicating official approval (or at least unwillingness to challenge the mobs).[29] When the plague struck Algeria in 1706, the ruler declared it to be the fault of the Jews and ordered the destruction of their synagogues and the confiscation of their property. In the late nineteenth century, Americans blamed Jews for importing the plague, typhus, and tuberculosis, which was called the "Jewish disease" or "tailor's disease," because tailoring appeared to be the profession of many Jewish immigrants [30]

An epidemic of typhus struck down 30,000 French troops besieging Naples in 1528, forcing the French to abandon the effort. The Neapolitans called it "the French pox"; the French called it the "Neapolitan disease." Venetians in the fifteenth century blamed the plague on Slavs and Albanians. In the sixteenth century, they blamed continuing epidemics on the arrival of the Marranos—Spanish or Portuguese Jews who were forced to convert to Christianity—or Jewish refugees who were expelled from Spanish territories in 1492.[31] Over the centuries, the world has witnessed epidemics of what were popularly called "the Hungarian disease," "the Indian disease," "the English sweats," "the Jewish disease," "the Polish disease," and "the Russian disease."

The yellow fever epidemic that struck Philadelphia in 1793 intensified the partisan politics of the new republic. Fearing a deep social revolution along the lines of the French Revolution, the Federalists blamed the epidemic on French refugees and pushed for a ban on immigration from France. Democratic-Republican merchants, who were more sympathetic to the revolution and who also benefited from trade with France, pushed back. The political differences extended to cures, with Alexander Hamilton asserting that he had been cured by taking quinine and drinking wine.[32] Americans in the nineteenth century blamed Irish immigrants for the waves of cholera that struck U.S. cities, which the accusers called the "Irish disease" because the Irish drank so much whiskey. In the early twentieth century, Americans blamed Italian immigrants for outbreaks of polio.[33]

During the plague epidemic that struck India in the 1890s, rumors spread among the Indians that the British had put snake venom in the water supply.[34] Muslim pilgrims traveling from all over the world to Mecca and back were frequently blamed for spreading disease, especially cholera, during the nineteenth century. Muslims, in turn, blamed Hindus for spreading syphilis. (Completing the circle, Hindus during the COVID-19 pandemic accused India's Muslims of deliberately spreading the virus by spitting on doctors and health workers.[35])

Following a long tradition of blaming Gypsies (the Romani) for poisons and plagues, the Italian government in 1910 launched a campaign to blame them for the reappearance of cholera in southern Italy. Police were ordered to prevent Gypsies from coming into the country. Authorities then announced that the outbreak in Apulia was caused by the arrival of caravans of Gypsies from Russia—a fabricated scenario that became part of the official history. Playing to popular prejudices, compliant newspapers reminded readers that Gypsies not only represented a health risk but were also thieves who stole children as well as property. Prefects ordered the arrest of Gypsies throughout the republic. These measures did not slow the spread of cholera but they diverted the wrath of angry citizens, who took matters into their own hands, attacking Gypsies, street vendors, and homeless persons whom they thought were Gypsies.[36]

The names given to epidemics can reflect unequal suffering. For example, in the 1890s, people in the West called the third plague pandemic, which killed 20 million people in India (95 percent of the total deaths worldwide) the *Oriental plague* or the *Asiatic pestilence*.[37] The names can reinforce existing prejudices and lead to medical conceits that contagions have racial preferences or that "superior" races have greater immunity. (A pathogen designed to kill certain "inferior" races or ethnic groups is a dream of white supremacists.)

An article in the January 1900 *Journal of the Sanitary Institute* discussing the plague in India noted, "No danger practically existed of plague spreading from India to Europe by sea, as the commercial intercourse between India and Empire is maintained by Europeans who belong to a superior class, and who have hitherto enjoyed an exceptional immunity from plague."[38] While the beginning of this observation may be assumed to refer to better sanitation measures, the last part suggests immunity based on racial biology.

Since cholera seemed to affect poor, crowded neighborhoods where clean water was unavailable and sanitation nonexistent, the more fortunate people in the upper classes concluded that the poor were victims of their own "filthy" habits. The persistence of the miasma theory of disease supported the idea. If disease was caused by a noxious atmosphere, then why did some people breathing the same poisoned fumes fall ill while others did not? The answer, some people reasoned, must lie in the bodies of the sufferers—to use today's medical terms, they had preexisting conditions that rendered them vulnerable. The difference in the nineteenth century thinking, however, was that the predisposing causes at that time were believed to reflect moral dissipation rather than just physical afflictions.[39]

A presumed craving for monkey meat led many to put the onus on Africans for the AIDS contagion. The stigma for spreading AIDS was later transferred to homosexuals, hemophiliacs, heroin addicts, and Haitians. The CDC's inclusion of Haitians as AIDS carriers reflected the fact that Haiti was the first country outside of Africa to suffer a serious outbreak, and the first case in the United States probably came from Haiti. As a result, Haitians living in the United States suffered from widespread discrimination in employment, education, and housing.[40]

Mexicans were blamed for the 2009 swine flu epidemic, which some people called the "Mexican flu" or "fajita flu." Anti-immigration propagandists in the United States described Mexican immigrants as pathogen-ridden "deadly time bombs."[41] One speculated that terrorists were using Mexican immigrants as walking germ-warfare weapons.[42] Some U.S. politicians called for closing the Mexican border.[43] In March 2020, the Trump administration invoked a World War II law that allowed the government to promptly deport migrants to stop the spread of a contagious disease. The Biden administration left the law known as Title 42 in place, but announced in April 2022, that it would wind down the controversial procedure in May.[44]

REINFORCING ANTI-CHINESE SENTIMENTS

Chinese immigrants to the United States experienced rampant racism and outbreaks of mob violence long before concerns were raised about epidemics. The primary tensions derived from economic competition. Imported in large numbers to build railroads and work in mines, Chinese laborers worked for lower wages than white laborers. But they also competed as prospectors in the California gold fields, and Chinese entrepreneurs saved their money and opened small businesses—laundries and restaurants. This did not threaten the upper classes, but it enraged those lower down the economic ladder. Murders and lynchings of Chinese immigrants were not uncommon, and there were some notable massacres by angry mobs.

Racist theories of medicine reinforced anti-Chinese sentiments. Health authorities in the late nineteenth century subscribed to the notion that white Europeans had greater genetic immunity to contagious diseases because of their race. Darker-skinned people—Africans, Indians, and other Asians—were said to suffer more from epidemics because they rejected Western civilization, lived in filth, and were addicted to vice.[45] The particular Chinese vices frequently mentioned were prostitution, gambling, and opium smoking—although prostitution and gambling were hardly Chinese imports, especially to the Barbary Coast of San Francisco. And Chinese brothels were patronized primarily by whites. Opium-smoking was indeed a Chinese import, but by the late nineteenth century, alcoholism and drug addiction had reached epidemic levels among white Americans.[46]

Substance abuse is still a problem. From 2005 to 2019, an average of 70,000 Americans died annually from "deaths of despair," which includes alcohol poisonings, drug overdoses, and suicide. The deaths were concentrated among middle-aged whites with less than a college education, with the unemployed and those no longer looking for work disproportionately represented.[47] A number of countries reported that alcohol consumption increased significantly during the COVID-19 pandemic. A 2020 RAND Corporation study noted that alcohol consumption had increased by 14 percent compared with the level before the pandemic.[48]

Reflecting popular prejudices and political expediency, the San Francisco Board of Health, organized in 1870, blamed the Chinese for every outbreak of disease that hit the city of San Francisco in the late nineteenth and early twentieth centuries.[49] According to an 1871 report, the Chinese were responsible because they were "inferior in organic structure, in vital force, and in the constitutional conditions of full development."[50] "Ignoring all laws of hygiene and sanitation," the report said, the Chinese "bred and dissemminated disease, thereby endangering the welfare of the state and of the nation." The Surgeon General of the United States in 1900 endorsed and added to this view, claiming in a report that the plague selectively attacked Asians, owing to their poverty and vegetarian diets.[51]

These same attitudes underwrote the expansion of Western empires in the nineteenth century. European populations asserted that it was the "white man's burden" to civilize indigenous peoples in Africa, Asia, and the Americas. Such attitudes also informed the mindset of officials dealing with the epidemics that affected Asian immigrant communities in the United States. Outbreaks of disease in Honolulu, San Francisco, and other American cities were more severe in Chinese communities, where poor workers lived in crowded conditions and had less access to safe drinking water or public sanitation systems.

Several of the twentieth-century flu epidemics did originate in China. These include the 1918 H1N1 pandemic and its successors. The 1957 pandemic of H2N2—like the 1918 flu, a respiratory virus—was labeled the "Asian flu." The 1968 pandemic of H3N2—another respiratory virus—was first identified in Hong Kong and therefore was given the name "Hong Kong flu." Some people called it "Mao flu." President Trump was following a well-established tradition when he insisted on labeling COVID-19 "the China flu" or "kung flu."[52] (The Internet was filled with an enormous array of terms for COVID-19, some of them intended to be humorous, many of them racial slurs.[53] This reinforced long-standing animosity toward all Asian immigrants and their descendants, but especially the Chinese.)

The COVID-19 pandemic has been accompanied by a sharp rise in attacks on Asian Americans, who have become the scapegoats for some people's anxiety and anger. In the United States, anti-Asian hate crimes increased by 149 percent in 2020,[54] and one study showed an increase of 164 percent in the first quarter of 2021.[55] Attacks on Asians have increased in Europe as well. These come at a time when hate crimes in general declined because the pandemic reduced the number of people present in public places where most of the crimes occur.

The attacks on Asians reflect no offense by the victims other than their race. Most of the attacks are verbal assaults or acts of vandalism, but some are violent physical attacks.[56] They are random, and they take place in public spaces. The violent attacks generally target women and the elderly—those least able to defend themselves. Not surprisingly, most of the attacks are occurring in cities with large Asian populations. The perpetrators are diverse. According to a preliminary analysis of recent cases by the New York City Police Department, mental illness appears to be a "common denominator" in a number of the cases.[57] In San Francisco, which has a large Asian American population, reported hate crimes against Asian Americans and Pacific Islanders increased by 567 percent, jumping from nine attacks in 2020 to sixty attacks in 2021.[58]

NATIVISTS VERSUS NEWCOMERS

The 1918 flu pandemic coincided with a major wave of immigration to the United States. Between 1880 and the mid-1920s, the United States added more than 23 million immigrants, which was equivalent to almost half of its 1880 population and almost half of its population growth during the period.[59] Most of the newcomers were not from Great Britain, Ireland, and Northern Europe, as they had been in previous years, but instead came from Southern and Eastern Europe. Many of those from Eastern Europe were Jews. Previously, Irish immigrants had been branded as importers of cholera in the early part of the nineteenth century. Immigrants arriving from Italy, Russia, and the Austro-Hungarian Empire were seen as potential carriers of a variety of diseases, including typhoid, plague, infantile paralysis, and tuberculosis.[60]

The confluence of high immigration and the flu pandemic provoked backlash among local citizens, although some historians claim that the pandemic did not generate the degree of race or class antagonism seen in history's earlier epidemics.[61] Even the Chinese evaded being blamed for the 1918 flu. However, the 1918 flu pandemic coincided with widespread mob attacks by whites on Black Americans during what came to be called the "Red Summer" of 1919. Race riots and lynchings spread across the country. Most of the assaults on Blacks occurred in northern cities, including Philadelphia, New York, and Chicago, where Blacks had immigrated in large numbers for economic reasons. And recently arrived Blacks were also blamed for spreading the dreaded flu, which was a contributing factor in the violence.[62]

The 1918 flu also contributed to nativist sentiments that manifested themselves in the dramatic growth of the Ku

Klux Klan following World War I. The new version of the Klan, which emerged in 1915 following the release of D. W. Griffith's epic silent film *The Birth of a Nation,* which romanticized the Klan during Reconstruction, expanded its targets to include not only African Americans but also immigrants, Jews, and Catholics as well as communists, socialists, liberals, and progressives.

By the 1920s, the Klan had grown to more than a million members, who paraded openly in Washington, D.C., and other cities. It was no longer a strictly Southern organization. States with the largest membership were Indiana, Ohio, Texas, Pennsylvania, Illinois, Oklahoma, New York, Michigan, Georgia, New Jersey, and Florida. Nearly half of the members were businessmen, salesmen, clerks, lawyers, and doctors.[63]

AN EXCUSE FOR ANTI-SEMITISM

Attacks on Jewish targets were already increasing in both the United States[64] and a number of European countries before the COVID-19 pandemic began.[65] They reached a high point in 2019 and they remained at a high level in 2020—and increased even further in some European countries. Most of the deadly attacks in Europe were carried out by Islamist extremists, whereas in the United States most were carried out by right-wing extremists.[66]

The COVID-19 pandemic prompted a new round of conspiracy theories linking Jews with the virus.[67] While the tropes remained much the same as those that circulated centuries before—Jews had caused the epidemic; Jews were profiting from its consequences; Jews celebrated the deaths of non-Jews—the recent dissemination of such allegations appears qualitatively different. During the epidemics of the Middle Ages, anti-Semitism was so deeply embedded in the Christian culture of the time that inciting action against the Jews would hardly have been necessary. The current dissemination of allegations linking Jews to the pandemic has the quality of a promotional project, intended to persuade, rather than exploiting a historically ingrained prejudice that is shared by a majority of people as it was in the Middle Ages.

It is a group project, global in reach but reflecting different motives and agendas. Anti-Semitic and anti-Israeli sources located in the Arab world, Iran, and Turkey, but also Twitter posts in the West, promoted the idea that the State of Israel, which many in the Middle East regard as an enemy, engineered the virus to kill off the Palestinians or weaken its Arab or Iranian foes. Christian extremists pointed to the epidemic's toll in Israel to reassure their base that Jews were being punished for their rejection of Jesus Christ. Neo-Nazis and white supremacists reminded followers and potential recruits that hating Jews lies at the core of their ideology.

EPIDEMICS AND RELIGIOUS FAITH

Sudden waves of random deaths caused by disease raise questions about faith. In times when modern science hardly existed and contagion was little understood, people saw calamities through the lens of their religious beliefs. Perhaps God was punishing people for widespread sin or inadequate devotion. Or was the suffering intended to be a test of their faith? Were the end-times forecast in the Bible near at hand, giving cause to rejoice? Or had God abandoned the victims? Did God even exist?

For religious leaders, epidemics pose both challenges and opportunities. Widespread, inexplicable death might erode faith in God, but public anxiety could also promote belief. Epidemics call forth active religious intervention. Wavering believers are admonished to accept God's will, prepare for the promise of an eternal afterlife, and concern themselves about their salvation.

Epidemics create a necessity to rally the faithful, gather the flock, reaffirm belief, demonstrate piety, pray for relief, rise above fear. For the faithful, epidemics call for assembly, collective study, worship, prayer meetings, celebrations of Mass, rogation, processions, the spiritual lift of group song. During the COVID-19 pandemic, such displays have often collided with social-distancing mandates and restrictions on mass gatherings. Church services are condemned as "super-spreader" events. Singing together spreads the virus.

Enforcement of restrictive measures has proved difficult and contentious. Secular societies see religious manifestations as a threat to community health, while worshippers worry more about their souls. Some believe that through group study and prayer they are protecting not only themselves but the entire community. They resist enforcement of public health measures, labeling them religious persecution—the imposition of Godless tyranny. At a minimum, for determined group-worshippers spirituality is emotionally cathartic. Worshippers were also angered by what they saw as a double standard during the summer of 2020, when demonstrators for social justice gathered to protest but worshippers were often barred from attending religious services.

In the United States—in many respects still a very Christian society—mandatory suspensions of church services provoked angry resistance. Battle lines were drawn and they mirrored political views. Israel's ultra-Orthodox Haredim, already resented by many secular Israelis because of the Haredi community's political privileges and government subsidies, provoked outrage by their blatant disregard for health measures during the pandemic.

Recognizing no authority other than the word of their own rabbis, the Haredim continued to hold large gatherings and refused to wear masks. As a result, the Haredi community suffered far more COVID-19 deaths, proportionately, than the rest of the population. The community comprises 12.5 percent of Israel's population but by early 2021 accounted for 28 percent of the COVID-19 cases.[68] (The Haredi community in New York has also been disproportionately affected.) Critics both inside and outside of Israel claim that the Haredim have prolonged the pandemic for all Israelis. Many Israelis hoped that the behavior of the Haredim during the pandemic would finally weaken their influence in national politics, just as the Black Death weakened the Catholic Church in the fourteenth century.[69]

The pandemic has created dilemmas for Muslims as well. Islam obliges the faithful to make the hajj, a pilgrimage to Mecca, at least once in their lifetime. Every year, millions of Muslims from all over the world make the trip to pray in the holy city during the last month of the Islamic calendar. It is one of the world's largest gatherings (2.5 million people made the hajj in 2019), making it a colossal super-spreader event. Iran, which was hard-hit by COVID-19, had a similar problem with its religious sites.

Health authorities have worried for more than a century about the role of the Muslim pilgrimage as a conduit for contagion. It is believed that cholera, which originated in India, spread along pilgrimage routes to Mecca. The disease appeared in Arabia for the first time in 1821 and it reappeared in 1831, when it killed 20,000 people. Subsequent outbreaks occurred regularly in Arabia throughout the rest of the nineteenth century. In each case, the outbreaks were followed by outbreaks elsewhere in the Middle East, North Africa, South and Southeast Asia, Turkey, and the Balkans, as pilgrims brought the disease back with them.

EFFECTS ON RELIGIOUS INSTITUTIONS

Large-scale outbreaks of disease were unsettling events that seemed to push people toward beliefs and behaviors beyond traditional religion when religious authority almost exclusively determined how people perceived the world. The Black Death had an enormous impact on the institution of the Church, which was not surprising. The high mortality was a reminder of imminent death and, like imminent execution, concentrated people's minds.

The plague undermined Church authority in a number of ways. Faith did not appear to protect the devout against the disease. The clergy were decimated, and standards for recruiting and training had to be lowered to obtain sufficient replacements, some of whose poor behavior further undermined Church authority. Some people embraced a more personal mysticism, or turned to alternate religious practices that the official Church condemned as heresy.[70]

How much the continuing outbreaks of plague may have contributed to the Protestant challenge to the Catholic Church is harder to judge. The late-fourteenth and fifteenth centuries were turbulent periods in Church history, with rival popes, direct involvement in wars on the Italian peninsula, and other factors contributing to the turmoil.

Subsequent epidemics resulted in heightened personal religiosity. In Catholic countries such as Italy, they prompted returns to the practice of taking religious statues out of the churches and parading them in processions to display faith and implore relief.[71] Although they border on idolatry, these practices persist during times of crisis. In Guatemala in the early 1960s, indigenous members of *cofradías*—groups of church laymen—removed a statue of the patron saint of the local church during a drought and placed it in a withering cornfield, where they vowed it would remain until rain came. It did rain shortly thereafter.

As in other aspects of people's response to epidemics, certain religious issues seem to recur. The difference today is that society has generally become more secular and a greater variety of religions are on offer; therefore, we see more diverse responses.[72]

One issue is the reason for an outbreak. Religious leaders divide on whether the outbreak of disease and increase in death reflects a purely natural phenomenon—viral or bacteriological—or is the result of an angry God intent on punishing a wicked society. We have seen this in the COVID-19 pandemic. There are also differences about whether an outbreak is a tribulation society must get through or a sign of the end-times.[73]

Group worship remains a fundamental expression of religious belief. Compliance with or resistance to bans on gatherings for religious purposes is another dividing line. Such bans can also be a divisive issue between Christians and other religions and those unaffiliated with any church. In the United States, 75 percent of white evangelical Protestants and 59 percent of white Catholics have favored exempting churches from bans on social gatherings during the COVID-19 pandemic. In contrast, 75 percent of unaffiliated persons and 67 percent of non-Christian religions oppose such exemptions.[74] It is a battle between body and soul.

Expressing a secular and purely utilitarian view, others point out that religious faith, including group gatherings, has utility in maintaining morale, is a useful coping mechanism, and helps in positive thinking, all of which have both social and individual value for fostering good mental health and overcoming illness.

Religious views can also affect how people view vaccination. Some devout individuals fear that vaccination is the "mark of the beast"—a sign of wickedness that will prevent acceptance into heaven. Many seek exemption from mandatory vaccination on religious grounds. In fact, the Catholic Church and many others support vaccination for moral reasons, and no major denomination—including the Christian Science church, whose members rely largely on prayer—officially opposes vaccination.[75] But the COVID-19 pandemic has seen an increase in the numbers of individuals who claim that vaccination is contrary to their religious beliefs, and some independent megachurches and pop-up anti-vax churches support them.

Online guides to writing religious exemption requests have also appeared. One of these was produced by Children's Health Defense, which is described as an anti-vaccination group rather than a religious organization.[76] The guide, however, advises those seeking to emphasize their religious beliefs rather than their personal, philosophical, or medical objections. It is difficult to distinguish between sincere religious objections and the use of religion to defend or advance medical, philosophical, or political beliefs—only the individual claimant may know for sure. It can, however, alter how people view religion. Does it turn faith into a tool for individual beliefs?

One possible effect of the COVID-19 pandemic could be the further atomization of faith into a purely individual and entirely idiosyncratic selection of beliefs, capable of remote practice without intermediation by an institutionalized religious authority. Although personal faith can exist with no outward display of piety and can easily be exercised remotely, it would not necessarily be any less authentic or sincere.

The role of religion in public life is an issue peculiar to contemporary American society. Despite official separation of church and state, religion has great influence on politics. And, increasingly, religious beliefs not only coincide with political views, but political views themselves seem to have become a kind of religion.[77] Politics have become the principal lens through which many people view the world. For some, political views are expressions of faith and therefore impervious to facts. Politics impose not only adherence to a strict orthodoxy but also a requirement for continued public pronouncements and behavior confirming one's fealty. The punishment is ex-communication—literally, exclusion from the communion of believers. Opposing political views are seen as downright evil. Our political divide is increasingly taking on the fervor of religious warfare. As in so many other social and psychological dimensions of the pandemic, these developments did not begin with COVID-19 but were accelerated by the pandemic and efforts to control it.

CONSPIRACY THEORIES AND MASS DELUSIONS

Conspiracy theories flourish during epidemics. During the Black Death, the people of southern France combined their hatreds to blame the plague on the Moorish king of Granada, who, they believed, paid the Jews to bribe lepers to kill off Christians by poisoning water supplies.[78] In nineteenth-century England, doctors were accused of using cholera to kill people for body parts.[79] Seeing that cholera affected mostly poorer people, rumors started that the disease was being deliberately spread by the upper classes to exterminate the poor.[80]

Reflecting anti-German sentiments during World War I, some saw the 1918 pandemic as a biological weapon released by German submarines.[81] Given that Germany was the first country to use chemical weapons in the war, this was not so far-fetched. Many people in the United States and the United Kingdom believed that the virus resulted from the use of aspirin, a drug invented and produced by the German pharmaceutical company Bayer, which during World War I developed and produced chemical weapons.

COVID-19 conspiracies are variations on, or combinations of, several basic themes. One is that the COVID-19 pandemic is a hoax, fabricated (or at least greatly exaggerated) by the government to exert greater control over its citizens. A second theme accepts the virus as real but attributes its origins to various dark forces. A third theme focuses on nefarious motives behind the promotion of vaccination.

As examples, some current conspiracy theorists assert that the virus is a Chinese plot or that 5G wireless signals trigger it. Europe saw a barrage of arson attacks on wireless towers in 2020.[82] Some argue that the pandemic is a hoax invented to coerce the population to accept vaccines containing microchips that will create a global identification system—which, in turn, will prepare the way for a global coup by hidden manipulators who secretly orchestrate world events. A similar conspiracy theory has been advanced that COVID-19 was intentionally introduced by global elites like the financier and philanthropist billionaire George Soros, Microsoft's cofounder Bill Gates, and the World Economic Forum founder and executive chairman Klaus Schwab, in order to defeat President Trump and control the world.[83] Still another conspiracy promoter asserts that vaccinations against COVID-19 are causing thousands of deaths, which are being concealed from the public. These deaths are not random but are the result of deliberately toxic vaccine batches being sent to Republican-dominated areas in the United States in order to cripple or kill off the conservative population.[84] In other words, the pandemic is biological warfare. Though not initially related to COVID-19, other conspiracy theories, such as QAnon, have exploited the pandemic and flourished.

Most of these conspiracy theories are reruns of past conspiracy theories, with the blanks filled in differently. To replace natural causes, they provide a villain or combinations of villains working together. The villains are previously identified outcasts, foreign foes, religious or class enemies, or the perennial secret elites who really rule the world. They seek profit or power or have genocidal goals. Political leaders know the truth but conceal it from the public.

APOCALYPTIC THINKING

Apocalyptic thinking is another component of the plague mentality. Many Christians see wars and other calamities as proof that we are in the end-times prophesized by the Bible. The end of the world is nigh. Judgment Day is at hand. For the devout, this is reassuring, as it brings them closer to the coming of the Messiah, the end of suffering, the resurrection of the righteous, and eternal life. Christians, Jews, and Muslims share similar basic ideas about a coming Golden Age, although there are variations between and within each corridor of belief.

The Christian perspective—in particular, Evangelicals' interpretation of the end-times—is the most prominent viewpoint in the United States: according to a 2013 poll, 41 percent of all U.S. adults, 54 percent of Protestants, and 77 percent of Evangelicals believe we are living in the end-times.[85] By a large margin, more Americans than people in any other economically advanced nation say that the COVID-19 pandemic has strengthened their religious faith.[86] Like everything else in the United States, end-times beliefs have become politically polarized. Paradoxically, those beliefs do not shift people's focus from this life to the hereafter, but rather appear to increase their political activism. This occurs among people in both political parties.[87]

Another dimension of end-times thinking can be found among the survivalists and preppers, who retreat to remote redoubts where they stockpile food and weapons for self-defense during the anticipated collapse of society. COVID-19 has increased their numbers.

Epidemics encourage hoarding. Fearing a shutdown during COVID-19, many Americans rushed to stock up on basic foodstuffs and other needed items. Hand sanitizer, toilet paper, and paper towels were swept off the shelves. The feeling was that adopting a simpler lifestyle and being prepared for future disasters would not be a bad thing. What if Amazon stopped delivering? Those who could do so also escaped to safer, remote locations. This was hardly a new phenomenon: kings and nobles did the same during previous plagues.

Preppers may share the end-times thinking of many Christians and put their faith in God, but whether motivated by Biblical prophecy or alarming daily news, they are primarily concerned about surviving natural disasters or manmade catastrophes. They prepare for what they see as the inevitable breakdown of society. They plan escape routes; build bunkers; select remote sites with an eye to defense; amass stockpiles of canned food, seeds, guns, and ammunition; and study martial arts to protect themselves and their families against marauding bands. Preppers can be found throughout the world, but they are particularly an American phenomenon that reflects American history, religiosity, values, and myths.

Survivalism reflects Americans' sense of rugged individualism and their unique affinity for firearms. It requires self-reliance—an American virtue—rather than dependence on government or community. Yet there is strength in numbers and in being surrounded by likeminded people. Some preppers seek safety in relocation to more remote parts of the country already inhabited by people whom they see as sharing their conservative Christian values—and who happen to be whiter, although some people of color are also preppers.

FRAYING SOCIAL COHESION

Lack of trust in institutions and other societal factors during a pandemic may, at least in part, have its origins in past epidemics. Cholera epidemics in nineteenth-century Europe stretched social cohesion and surfaced latent social antagonisms. Some historians declare that these effects were transient.[88]

The 1918 flu pandemic suggests that this might not always be the case. The flu preceded the invention of antiviral drugs. There was no vaccine and no treatment. Those who caught the flu faced a high risk of death. Panic was widespread. Health officials in the state of Kentucky reported people "starving to death not from lack of food, but because the well were panic stricken and would not go near the sick."[89]

Unlike most other flus, which take the heaviest toll on the very young and the very old, the 1918 flu put young adults at greatest risk of death. A combination of the flu, public health measures, and continuous advisories to avoid interpersonal contacts contributed to "a profound climate of suspicion and mistrust."[90] The fact that the flu affected young adults more severely than other elements of society "increased the ability of the pandemic to disrupt the social tissue."[91] But how long do these effects last?

Recent research suggests that the 1918 flu had broad and *long-lasting* societal impacts.[92] The methodology and mathematics behind this finding are complicated, but it indicates that the social disruption caused by the 1918 flu significantly eroded people's trust, and—the most fascinating finding—this lack of trust was inherited by descendants. The researchers, based in Milan, Italy, started with two basic ideas: First, social attitudes, including trust, are shaped by both the contemporary environment and by inherited beliefs and norms—in other words, trust and distrust are, at least to some extent, inherited. Second, the constant encouragement by the authorities during the Spanish flu for people to avoid interpersonal contacts (which could lead to death) fueled lasting wariness.

The Italian researchers used the General Social Survey (GSS), which is the most comprehensive survey of changing attitudes in America and allows comparisons over an eighty-year time frame, to explore this issue in 2021. Specifically, they wanted to know how respondents answered one key question: "Generally speaking, would you say that most people can be trusted or that you can't be too careful in dealing with people?"

The GSS did not allow researchers to connect individual responses with family experience, but they were able to compare answers with the national origins of family ancestors who came to the United States after the 1918 flu. This provided an indirect way to connect the attitudes of

American offspring with the experience of their parents, grandparents, and great-grandparents.

They found that respondents whose ancestors emigrated from countries that had suffered high mortality rates from the disease—in particular, from countries that were neutral during World War I and therefore did not censor news of the outbreak, which began in the last year of the war—were the most mistrustful compared to those whose ancestors came from less-affected countries. This inherited distrust persisted decades after the pandemic.

Although the evidence is necessarily more anecdotal, it is in line with previous research on the Black Death and the nineteenth-century cholera epidemics, which also inflicted long-lasting damage on personal trust, damage that affected following generations.

Epidemics also contribute to a coarsening of society. It is unrealistic to expect courtesy to prevail when people are surrounded by widespread death and their own survival is in doubt, but that hardly describes the situation of most people in America or Europe during the COVID-19 pandemic. Civility has been declining for decades for a variety of reasons, and the pandemic has added new layers of edginess, including confrontations over mask-wearing, which political leaders have fomented.[93] There is not just a loss of comity but an increase in aggression.

Psychologists blame the observed increase in antisocial behavior during the pandemic—actions that violate the rights of others or are disruptive to society—on prolonged isolation, which heightens anxiety, increases irritability, promotes aggression, and diminishes impulse control. Essentially, people have shorter fuses. The

United States is especially vulnerable, since one in three Americans lives alone, but the United Kingdom and other countries in Europe have observed similar trends. The effects may be hard to reverse.[94]

Epidemics cause stress, which in turn limits a person's ability to restrain impulses. Much of the random violence, seen especially at markets, in restaurants, and on airplanes and other public transportation, where people are surrounded by strangers, appears to be unplanned outbursts in response to immediate circumstances. But it also reflects an underlying anger. Chronic stress provokes "displaced aggression"—anger released on someone who has nothing to do with the original source of the provocation.[95]

Reckless and nihilistic behavior also accompanies epidemics and it can, in turn, foster an erosion of ethics and a decline in respect for the law. It derives from the notion that there are no consequences to lawless or destructive behavior. As Thucydides noted in his horrific account of the 430–429 B.C.E. epidemic that killed up to a third of Athens's population, and its immediate aftermath, the sudden wave of deaths left disorder in its wake:

> Athens owed to the plague the beginnings of a state of unprecedented lawlessness. Seeing how quick and abrupt were the changes of fortune which came to the rich who suddenly died and to those who had previously been penniless but now inherited their wealth, people now began openly to venture on acts of self-indulgence . . . As for the gods, it seemed to be the same thing whether one worshipped them or not, when one saw the good

and the bad dying indiscriminately. As for offenses against human law, no one expected to live long enough to be brought to trial and punished.[96]

The massive death tolls of medieval pandemics cheapened life, which was already cheap, especially for those at the bottom of the social pyramid. Some suggest that this led to increases in murder, although other historians challenge this thesis.[97] Following a later round of the Black Death, which struck Italy particularly hard in 1630, the erosion of social norms and hierarchy led to an outbreak of homicidal violence. The 1918 flu reportedly also prompted an increase in murder-suicides resulting from depression. "Newspapers on both sides of the Atlantic carried stories of men and women who attempted to slay their families."[98]

Using data from 1918, research shows that social distancing was a good predictor of the suicide rate.[99] Although national data for the years before, during, and immediately after the 1918 flu pandemic are imperfect, since only a few states reported suicide statistics in the early twentieth century, World War I actually may have reduced the suicide rate, because wars tend to unite society. However, according to the research, the suicide rate in the United States increased during the later months of the flu. It is likely that the physical and social distancing associated with the pandemic contributed to the increase. The flu led to the closing of saloons, the curtailment of open political campaigning, and self-isolation. Fear of the virus and grief over the loss of loved ones may also have been factors.[100]

Coming back to the COVID-19 pandemic, suicide rates in the United States, which had been climbing since 2000, actually declined in 2020, although twice as many people reported that they had thought about committing suicide. Whether the downward trend in 2020 continues or the increased number of people thinking about ending their own lives presages an increase in suicides must await the compilation of the 2021 statistics.

VIOLENT CRIME

Increases in crime have accompanied many of the previous epidemics in history, from the Athenian epidemic to the Black Death to the cholera epidemics of the nineteenth century to threats to law and order during the 1918 flu early in the twentieth century. Reports early in the COVID-19 pandemic (April 2020) indicated a decline in ordinary street crime but "dramatic increases in domestic violence and abuse."[101] Later reports showed that domestic violence climbed by 60 percent in Europe, and in the United States homicides increased by more than 29 percent, to more than twenty thousand, for the first time since 1995. The 2020 murder surge was the largest increase in violence in the United States since 1960.[102] Worldwide statistics indicate that domestic or "intimate partner" violence increased between 25 and 33 percent worldwide.[103]

Americans bought 23 million guns in 2020,[104] an increase of 65 percent over the number bought in 2019. Mass shootings (i.e., shootings in which four or more persons are shot) increased in the United States by 46 percent in 2020.[105] Figures for 2021 show 818 mass shootings resulting in 920 deaths versus 696 mass shootings with 661 killed in 2020.

In addition to homicides, violent confrontations and

random assaults (attacks on strangers) have increased during the pandemic. As is usually the case, certain venue categories, such as public transportation, commercial aviation, schools, and hospitals, offer clues to broader developments in society. This is not because a particular venue is necessarily the target but because these are places where the public comes together in a defined space and security concerns mean that statistics are maintained.

A number of cities have reported an increase in random assaults.[106] Some of these involve stabbings or slashing attacks. Incidents involving unruly passengers on commercial airliners—often disorderly drunks but sometimes violent assaults on crew or passengers—have been a growing international problem for years. The U.S. Federal Aviation Administration reported a dramatic increase in serious incidents between January and November 2021, when there were 5,114 unruly-passenger reports leading to 973 investigations.[107] Anecdotal evidence suggests an increase in attacks on public surface transportation as well, which also has been a long-term trend. It must be noted that ridership on public transportation dropped dramatically during the pandemic shutdowns in 2020 but it increased in 2021 as restrictions eased. The apparent increase in attacks has to be adjusted for increased ridership.

Students returning to in-person classes saw a significant increase in fights, riots, and attacks on teachers and staff. In August and September 2021, a total of fifty-six instances of gunfire on school grounds were recorded.[108] Confrontations, some violent, also extended to school board and parent-teacher meetings.

Assaults at hospitals also increased by more than 23 percent in 2020. (Figures are not yet available for 2021.) These were "non-aggravated" assaults—that is, assaults with no or only minor injuries. At the same time, there was a 24 percent increase in disorderly conduct.[109]

While these statistics pertain to North America, similar trends have been observed in Europe. Much of the unruly behavior appears to be a consequence of the socially and psychologically upsetting effects of the pandemic. A lot of it is directly related to angry confrontations over mask mandates. That would suggest that antisocial violence should decline as the pandemic fades. However, an increase in brutish behavior may be a lasting legacy of the pandemic.

The pandemic is not the only cause of the surge in violence in the United States. Gun purchases surged in June and July 2020, following widespread protests over the police killing of George Floyd, and again from November 2020 to January 2021, following the disputed presidential election.[110]

However, the protests—the vast majority of which were peaceful—do not explain the increase in homicides. Of the more than twenty thousand homicides in the United States in 2020, approximately twenty-five to thirty may have been connected with the protests, but the connections are not always clear. A review of twenty-seven deaths of individuals who died during the protests shows that some were killed by gun owners who claimed to be defending themselves or their property against protesters and looters. Others were killed by the police or National Guard soldiers. Counterprotesters were responsible for killing several individuals. Few of the deaths are known to have been caused by the protesters themselves.[111]

The COVID-19 pandemic may have contributed to the increase in violent deaths in a number of ways. Shutdowns meant more people spending more time at home, which could increase domestic violence. People out of work had more time on their hands. Hospitals already crowded with patients may have been unable to treat the sick or people wounded or injured in violent attacks; other persons needing care avoided hospitals, fearing contagion. It is too early to say whether the observed trends in crime will turn out to be temporary aberrations, reflecting the unique circumstances of the pandemic, or that they presage a more lasting change in the trajectory of American violence.

ORGANIZED CRIME

During the COVID-19 pandemic, fundamental shifts have occurred in the realm of organized crime. Like other commercial enterprises, criminal organizations have had to deal with disruptions of their operations, including reductions in income from extortion and protection rackets as businesses shut down, interruptions in supply chains needed for the processing of illegal drugs, and breakdowns of distribution channels. At the same time, however, the pandemic has created new opportunities that criminal organizations, more agile than governments, can exploit.

Drug cartels faced with shortages of precursor chemicals to refine cocaine have shifted to the manufacture of methamphetamine or fentanyl. Quick to exploit dislocations and scarcities in the economy, organized crime operates black markets. In some countries, criminal enterprises are involved in the supply of scarce medical supplies to the wealthy. Already engaged in the manufacture and distribution of counterfeit pharmaceuticals, criminal organizations have moved into the production of fake COVID-19 tests and vaccines, fake vaccination certificates, and other pandemic-related areas.[112]

International criminal rings have siphoned billions of dollars from pandemic relief funds.[113] Cybercrime, which has been increasing over the years, further increased during the pandemic.[114] However, it was growing rapidly before the pandemic, and how much of the recent increase is a result of the pandemic is unknown. Isolation has resulted in more people shopping on the Internet, which has increased opportunities for cybercrime. There also have been reports of ransomware attacks on hospitals.

The plight of many small businesses that face bankruptcy and cannot get loans from legitimate sources creates new opportunities for loan-sharking, a traditional business of organized crime. Loans at usurious rates provide continuing income and also offer an opportunity for organized crime to launder money—and in many cases take over businesses entirely.

With increased border controls and restrictions on immigration that are likely to persist after the pandemic subsides, migrant smuggling is likely to become a bigger business. It is already highly profitable but it currently appears to be a decentralized service industry. Increasing demand and greater risks will require more-sophisticated operations—a growth area for organized crime.[115]

Widespread unemployment will increase the reservoir of recruits willing to join criminal enterprises. At the very least, economic desperation may increase social tolerance of criminal activities, especially as the pandemic has exposed not only government incompetence and corruption but also the inherent unfairness of political and economic systems. Less respect for government means less respect for the law.

The popular image of gangsters perpetually at war with government is misleading. Murders, assassinations, and shootouts with police and other gangs are just one facet of organized crime. Criminal enterprises routinely resort to violent coercion but they also rely on complicity and collaboration and they compete with government for popular support.

John Sullivan and Robert Bunker have compiled an informative series of essays exploring how cartels and other criminal organizations in various parts of the world have responded to the COVID-19 pandemic.[116] The case studies illustrate not merely purely criminal actions but also the political dimensions of competition with government for control and consent of the people, especially in developing countries.

In some countries, competing criminal organizations have negotiated truces with each other, and even with government, to concentrate on the health crisis. In several countries, criminal organizations are enforcing quarantines and other public health measures in areas they control. In a number of cases, cartels and mafias are directly providing humanitarian aid—food packages and other necessities—sometimes delivered in branded boxes carrying the provider's name and logo.

The concept of social banditry, which portrays crime as social resistance supported by wider society and therefore moral and acceptable, albeit illegal—essentially, criminals perceived as Robin Hoods—should not be overstated.[117] The primary goal of a criminal gang is profit, not fulfilling a social contract. However, social control measures and charitable relief during times of natural disaster and distress enable criminal enterprises to "wedge themselves into the socioeconomic framework,"[118] creating a parallel system of loyalty and authority and making them difficult to root out.

The COVID-19 pandemic is an immense experience shared by humankind. It has penetrated all corners of the globe, caused dramatic increases in deaths, disrupted lives, and caused social alienation and widespread apprehension. Post-traumatic stress disorder (PTSD) is an individual diagnosis, but societies can collectively display symptoms of anxiety, hypervigilance, suspicion, belligerence, aggressive behavior. Some of these effects will fade along with the pandemic and a return to some kind of normality, but many of the observed behaviors reflect pre-pandemic trends. We are unlikely to see a return to the way we were before—*status quo ante pestilentiam*. The post-pandemic world will be a different world.

TURNING THE PAGE

Thus far, we have conducted a damage assessment. The death toll and economic effects of the COVID-19 pandemic can be quantified, although not precisely. And the economic recovery can be projected over the next several years, although the charts may imply greater certainty than actually exists. The pandemic's effects on society are more insidious. They can be identified but not calibrated, nor do we know how they may alter our outlook and lives in the coming years.

The next section examines how the demographic, economic, and societal effects of the pandemic might affect the political future. Will the pandemic doom already fragile governments? Will it shatter the social order, or will it strengthen the hand of oppression? Will it lead to increased unrest and civil disorder, as has occurred at times in the past? Could it bring about armed conflict, new terrorism campaigns, civil wars? Increased violence, brigandage, rebellions, and wars have followed in the wake of previous epidemics, which is not to say that they were caused by the epidemics or that past trajectories will be replicated in the wake of the current pandemic. History merely provides clues; it does not mark a path.

CHAPTER 4:
POLITICAL
REPERCUSSIONS

FROM THE BLACK Death to the COVID-19 pandemic, epidemics have been accompanied and followed by civil disobedience, social unrest, violent protests, increases in communal violence, armed uprisings, rebellions, and war. Epidemics have not only killed people, they have brought down governments and ended dynasties.

Confucian scholars in ancient China promoted the idea that the ruler of a state was established by heaven for the benefit of the people. The ruler kept the Mandate of Heaven to rule "only so long as he retained the support of the people, for it was through the 'heart' of the people that Heaven made its will known."[1] Calamities like drought, famine, and plague were seen as signs that the ruler had lost the mandate and required replacement. People could rightfully hold their ruler to account. Challenges were legitimate. Emperors fell.

Writing at the height of the first wave of the COVID-19 pandemic, my friend and former colleague at the RAND Corporation, Francis Fukuyama, observed that a "lingering epidemic combined with deep job losses, a prolonged depression, and an unprecedented debt burden will inevitably create tensions that turn into political backlash—but against whom is as yet unclear."[2]

The pandemic proved tenacious. By the spring of 2022, the fifth wave, caused by the Omicron variant that swept across the world in January and February, was declining. But a possible sixth wave, pushed by a subvariant of the Omicron variant, was again increasing the number of new cases toward 2 million a day worldwide, and about 30,000 a day in the United States. It appears that the world confronts a long slog, especially in areas where mitigation measures are difficult and vaccination is proceeding very slowly. The United States, Europe, and East Asia are recovering economically, though some sectors are still struggling. After spiking in 2020, unemployment in the United States and Europe has rapidly declined and is approaching pre-pandemic levels. Again, developing countries are recovering more slowly. Political tensions have increased.

POLITICAL CASUALTIES

The COVID-19 pandemic has already seen some political casualties. Fate, not fraud, destroyed President Trump's re-election bid. Under ordinary circumstances, a powerful incumbent presiding over a robust economy and low unemployment would have been hard to beat. The pandemic quickly wiped out the economic gains and led to massive unemployment. The president initially dismissed the disease, then continually diminished its danger, belittling his own health officials for what he considered overreacting. For President Trump, the level of the stock market was a continuous validation of his successes. Protecting the economy took precedence over public health concerns, delaying a response, allowing the contagion to spread in the first crucial days. Trump lost the election. The pandemic has also taken a political toll on President Biden who, during the campaign, blamed his predecessor for the many deaths suffered during the pandemic and—in a moment of political hubris—rashly promised, "I will end this." It was foolhardy. Despite efforts to impose stronger safety protocols, accelerate vaccinations, and increase the availability of masks and test kits, COVID-19 deaths in the United States more than doubled during the new president's first year in office, and fairly or not, he was held accountable. At the same time, the Biden administration's efforts to contain the spread of the virus by mandating masks and vaccination provoked widespread protests.

The president of Peru and the prime minister of Italy were brought down in part by the pandemic. The United Kingdom's prime minister, Boris Johnson, was put under police investigation and faced a political scandal—which the press labeled "partygate"—over parties at 10 Downing Street in violation of pandemic control measures. The Brazilian senate recommended that President Jair Bolsonaro be indicted for criminal offenses, including crimes against humanity, for his mishandling of the COVID-19 pandemic, which has resulted in Brazil suffering one of the highest per capita death rates in the world. The prime minister of India faced increased anger as a result of soaring COVID-19 cases and the failures of the country's medical system. While the number of cases in India subsided during the second half of 2021, it surged in Russia, reaching its highest point ever in October, contradicting President Putin's earlier claims that Russia was coping with COVID-19 better than most countries.[3] Colombian President Iván Duque's attempt to solve the country's pandemic-caused debt problem by raising taxes provoked nationwide protests against his government, as well as continuing violence.[4]

Like the fourteenth-century rulers who tried to make up revenue lost to the plague, the Colombian government sought to reduce a deficit in government income after COVID-19 reduced the country's gross domestic product by 6.8 percent. To people already suffering from increased unemployment and fearing being pushed into poverty, the tax increase was intolerable, and thousands took to the streets. The government forbid the protests on health grounds and deployed a heavy police presence, which escalated the violence and the protesters' demands.[5] The government responded by deploying the military to suppress the disturbances. This does not affect Duque's political fortunes, however. Since 2015, Colombia's president cannot run for reelection.

These early political confrontations and casualties are part of a historical pattern. The Confucian concept of the Mandate of Heaven, even when less poetically described, has broader application. In Western history, rulers might have claimed to rule by divine right, but widespread misfortune—famine, war, pestilence—eroded faith in leadership. Unlucky rulers were vulnerable.

Perceptions that callous, incompetent, or corrupt officials had made things worse further undermined political legitimacy. The Black Death decimated European officialdom, crippling the bureaucracies that collected taxes, administered the law, and ran the everyday machinery of government. Hastily recruited replacements were inexperienced, untrained, less competent, and often dishonest. Protests against inefficiency and corruption were widespread in Europe during the second half of the fourteenth century.[6]

There is no straight line from the cholera epidemics that struck Russia beginning in the 1830s to the Russian Revolution, but the outbreaks of disease and the accompanying cholera riots contributed to the growing social and political tensions of the nineteenth century that erupted in 1917. The deliberate delay in announcing that cholera was present in Hamburg's water supply, and further delays in voting funds to combat the spread of the disease, resulted in the "moral discrediting" of the Hamburg government in 1892.[7]

The cholera outbreak in Naples in 1884, and especially the outbreak in 1911, posed a major political challenge to the government of Italy. The country had been unified only since 1870. Unification had brought little benefit to southern Italy, and the region remained restive—and, from Rome's perspective, politically dangerous. The return of cholera to Naples and Sicily created a national political crisis. The government's initial response to the epidemic was a denial of the outbreak, publication of fake statistics, and the use of "repressive means to impose a veil of silence."[8] As Frank Snowden noted in his masterful history *Naples in the Time of Cholera, 1884–1911*, "The process of moral erosion, once established, proved irreversible. The cholera epidemic of 1911 was one more instance of the way in which the disregard for the law and the constitution created an atmosphere of suspicion and disrespect surrounding the state."[9] Failures of government in response to epidemics would have terrible consequences a decade later.

The AIDS epidemic destroyed tourism in Haiti in the early 1980s, pushing the already impoverished country into deeper poverty. The loss of tourism was not the only reason for the fall of Jean-Claude Duvalier in 1986 but its consequences clearly contributed.[10] In light of the devastating impact of COVID-19 on global tourism, countries already suffering from ineffectual or corrupt rule and dependent on tourism for a large share of their income will be on a political crisis watchlist.

While epidemics have not always directly caused the downfall of governments, in some cases they have produced an illumination effect. Just as contracting a disease may expose a host of underlying health conditions that may weaken a patient's resistance and ultimately lead to his or her demise, the glare of mass deaths illuminates the underlying ills of a society. What may have seemed unremarkable, even tolerable in normal times, becomes insufferable.

As Richard Evans observes in his monumental study of the 1892 cholera epidemic in Hamburg, "The structures of social inequality, the operations of political power, the attitudes and habits of mind of different classes and groups in the population, come to light with a clarity of profile unimaginable in more normal times."[11]

Like previous major epidemics, the COVID-19 pandemic has flayed the body politic, laying bare its acute social tensions, economic divides, racial prejudices, political disfunction, and inherent frailties. The pandemic has aggravated these preexisting conditions, undermined government credibility, provoked defiance, and demonstrated the limits of government authority when faced with widespread public resistance. The pandemic also created new models of resistance, like the truck convoys that blocked bridges between Canada and the United States, clogged downtown Ottawa, and circled Washington, D.C.

DEMOCRACY OR POPULISM

For the first time in many years, progress toward democracy declined in 2020, wiping out fifteen years of gain. This happened not simply because many governments increased controls in response to the pandemic but because—according to the Economist Intelligence Unit's Democracy Index—many governments exploited the health emergency to erode democratic gains.

Democracy itself lost some of its luster. Democracies struggled to control the spread of COVID-19. As of December 2021, only 39 percent of the world's twenty-three "full democracies" experienced per capita mortality rates below the global median, while 61 percent had mortality rates above the median—eight of the twenty-three countries had per capita mortality rates more than twice the world average. (The United States is not included in the twenty-three, as it is categorized in the index as a "flawed democracy.")[12] As of December 2021, the United States and Europe (minus Russia and Ukraine), which account for just 11 percent of the world's population, had experienced nearly 36 percent of the world's COVID-19 fatalities. The United States alone experienced more than 15 percent of the world's total COVID-19 fatalities.

There are several possible explanations for this. First, these are not the final numbers. The pandemic is still surging in many countries, and COVID-19 deaths are not accurately reported in many parts of the world. The democracies also tend to be more urbanized, densely populated, and interconnected, conditions that facilitate contagion. Nonetheless, the optics are undeniable. It is not that the world's democracies or economically advanced countries have fared a lot worse than other countries—although in some cases that is clearly the case—it is that they have not obviously done better. Will this lead to more lasting damage to their influence?

Democracies' struggle against the pandemic does not mean that populist regimes have done especially well. In fact, initial figures suggest that populist leaders have performed significantly worse than traditional politicians in dealing with COVID-19. The United States, Brazil, India, Mexico, Peru, the United Kingdom, Italy, Russia, France, and Colombia comprise the top ten hardest-hit countries in terms of total deaths. When the pandemic began, all except France were governed by leaders who were described as populists.

Populist leaders have tended to downplay the pandemic, dramatize their own responses, and assert their own views and solutions, in many cases dismissing the advice of their own medical and public health advisors or replacing those advisors with officials who were more in line with their personal opinions.[13] It is classic populist behavior that sharpens political differences and polarizes populations.

Microbes have no politics. Epidemics do not directly create conflict; they run along existing political, economic, and social fault lines to accentuate tensions and stoke political strife. As we have seen in previous outbreaks of disease, existing cleavages become political battlefronts between national and local authorities, monarchs and free cities, political authority and commercial elites, the wealthy and the poor, the public good and individual liberty. There are numerous examples of political authorities combining forces with commercial interests during the later pandemics and cholera outbreaks of the nineteenth century—in German, British, Italian, and American cities—to protect commerce against controls favored by health officials.

Epidemics divide communities along racial, ethnic, class, and political lines. They provide fertile ground for demagogues and rabble-rousers, racists and nativists, political and religious fanatics.

Every aspect of an epidemic becomes a battleground: acceptance or denial of its existence; acceptance of or resistance to quarantines, shutdowns, social distancing, face masks, and other preventive measures aimed at suppressing the disease. In the case of COVID-19, face-mask rules, vaccination, vaccination mandates, and vaccination passports have become highly contentious issues. The role of the state itself is questioned.

The disputes overlap, creating a mosaic of alliances and adversaries. Although California's whites—from tycoons to ordinary laborers—were generally hostile to Chinese immigrants in 1900, when faced with an outbreak of the plague, city officials, commercial interests, and Chinese merchants and workers quarantined in the city's Chinatown saw common cause against the strict lockdown. The leading Chinese merchants in the city brought a federal lawsuit demanding that the quarantine be lifted on the grounds that it was highly discriminatory—and the judge agreed.

At the same time, California's business community and the state's governor appealed directly to the White House to remove the local head of the federal Marine Hospital Service, whose concern about the spread of plague had persuaded him to impose strict control measures that threatened the city's reputation and the state's economy. The governor also ordered that state health authorities be present at all autopsies conducted by federal officials to make their own determination as to whether plague was the cause of death. Needless to say, these clashes hindered collaborative efforts to eradicate or mitigate the outbreak.[14]

Events during the 1900 plague foreshadowed the angry public disputes that have accompanied control measures and vaccination efforts prompted by the COVID-19 pandemic. Confrontations between citizens, principally over mask mandates, have led to increasingly violent rhetoric, causing the Department of Homeland Security to warn that extremists could exploit the reimposition of COVID-19 restrictions as a rationale for violent attacks.[15]

Historically, these tensions reflected self-interest, and sometimes political opportunism, but they often also represented fundamentally different political philosophies. We will avoid malleable terms like *liberal*, *conservative*, or *progressive*—their meaning shifts with time and place. The basic question is: Which takes priority—

the well-being of the state or the protection of its citizens?

As Richard Ross points out in his study of the 1831 cholera epidemic in Prussia, that experience led to a review of how the country would deal with infectious diseases in the future. The new policy

> addressed the congruent needs of government officials sympathetic to the economic interests of the middle class that they saw as critical to the future economic welfare of the state. For the Prussian bourgeoisie the highest priorities at the time were political and economic in nature . . . They supported a "liberal" ideology that promoted more personal and economic freedom. The middle class was not prepared to support an interventionist medically based social policy that they would have seen as leading to more government interference and required coercive enforcement.[16]

Commenting on this approach after a typhus epidemic struck Silesia in 1848, one Prussian physician noted that "civil servants had not been appointed to serve their [typhus victims'] interests, rather they were appointed by the police state to serve the interests of the state."[17] Variations of battles reflecting different political views were also apparent during the cholera epidemics and the third plague pandemic in Europe and the United States.

In an existential war, it would be accepted that many might die to ensure the survival of the state. If one views an epidemic as existential war, casualties to protect the well-being of the state may be more acceptable. In epidemics, the state's well-being is generally defined in terms of economic health, which means opposition to anything that restricts commerce, impedes trade, or gets in the way of the availability of labor. This definition corresponds to business interests but it is seen and portrayed in political terms as individual liberty, and it is the good of the country—essentially meaning the good of the dominant economic elites—that is paramount.

Others would define the good of the country in terms of the survival and welfare of its population. Accordingly, the priority must be saving lives, even if that means interrupting commerce to do so. The medical community and health officials are dedicated—and many doctors are bound by their Hippocratic Oath—to emphasizing their patients' interests; in other words, the paramount objective is to save lives, even if that means accepting collateral damage to the economy.

The basic differences between the two views can lead to complex interpretations. For example, in debates about the current pandemic, the issue of elderly Americans has occasionally arisen, especially at the beginning of the pandemic. Because of their age and the fact that they often have underlying health conditions, they are the most vulnerable members of society, accounting for a majority of deaths from COVID-19 (and, earlier, for ordinary seasonal increases in flu). In medical terms, that makes them a priority concern and a major reason for social distancing, shutdowns, and vaccination.

Some, however, have questioned why the country should suffer unnecessary economic harm, or children be deprived of normal education by the closing of schools, in order to protect those who require a disproportionate share of precious health-care resources—space in intensive care units and vaccines. Is it the patriotic duty of the elderly to accept greater risk in order to protect the able-bodied young and future generations?

It is a tricky ethical question that epidemics predating modern medicine did not confront. The absence of effective medical treatment and vaccines meant that an epidemic ran its course. Often, the weakest due to age, inadequate living conditions, access to clean water, and malnutrition died in greater numbers. So did the very young. In the COVID-19 pandemic, the United States has given first priority to "critical health-care and other workers" deemed essential for national survival. The second tier comprises those who also work in health care or essential jobs. In other words, the imperative is to maintain the country's ability to deal with the health crisis while keeping essential services running. Those 65 and older are included in the third tier. The general population makes up the final two tiers. The youngest have not suffered the high levels of mortality common with other diseases.

The pandemic has exposed shortcomings in the ability of hospitals to handle surges of the disease. The provision of medical care—especially in the United States—has yielded to market forces. To remain profitable, hospitals have to be lean and efficient, a sort of just-in-time approach to public health. Many hospitals had closed during previous decades, reducing the ability of the nation to deal with sudden surges. Shutdowns to slow the spread of the virus have been considered necessary to prevent treatment capacity from being overwhelmed.

Vaccines were produced and distributed quickly enough to compress the differences between the times when different tiers of the population became eligible for vaccination. However, in less-developed countries, where only a small percentage of the people have been vaccinated and vaccines remain in short supply, ethical questions of who goes first may be contentious.

PUBLIC DISORDERS

Public disorders both preceded and followed the Black Death in fourteenth-century Europe. Strikes and urban uprisings "against city oligarchies and mayors, changes in monetary policy, rises in house rents, the privileges and impositions of the crown, and above all against the imposition of new taxes" were common in France and Flanders during the decades before the first wave of the plague in 1347.[18] Peasant revolts occurred frequently. Italy saw clashes that pitted those without citizenship or political status, commoners, wool workers, weavers, merchants, shopkeepers, and artisans against landed and mercantile aristocracies in continuing class warfare that sometimes led to the overthrow of local regimes.

The uprisings were local and differed between northern and southern Europe. Beginning about a decade after the emergence of the Black Death, the pattern began to change. Propelled by economic distress, along with roaming bands of desperate men turned bandits and the imposition of new taxes as royal governments and local nobles sought to make up lost revenue caused by the continuing onslaught of the plague, rebellions occurred frequently throughout Europe and continued into the next century. Samuel Cohn counted more than five hundred revolts in Italy alone during this period.[19]

The later struggles were more intense than the earlier ones. Popular outrage focused on the concrete issue of taxes and abuses by the aristocracy. The language of opposition became more political, not merely addressing a specific injustice but challenging the political order.[20]

In England, the arrival of the Black Death in 1347 triggered a chain of events that led to a mass movement and the country's first popular social revolution in 1381. The initial wave of the plague wiped out nearly half of the population. Subsequent waves in 1361, 1369, and 1375 further reduced the population to 2.5 million, 45 percent of what it had been when the plague first struck. This resulted in an acute shortage of labor that enabled peasant workers to bargain for higher wages. Alarmed by the economic shift and the impudence of the commoners, the crown imposed strict wage and price controls, reinforced requirements to provide labor as required by the lords, and even prohibited the lower classes from wearing clothes above their social rank.

Repeated waves of plague were not the only source of hardship. Agricultural production was hindered by climate change and extreme weather events in the form of exceptional cold spells and heavy rains that led to harvest failures. Contagious diseases also caused huge die-offs of cattle and sheep.[21] Meanwhile, the mounting financial demands of England's costly war with France added to political tensions.

To generate new sources of desperately needed revenue, the government imposed poll taxes—fixed amounts that hit the poor hardest—provoking resistance against the unfairness of the system and the corruption of the king's officers. Local uprisings coalesced into the Peasants' Revolt of 1381. Thousands marched on London and briefly seized control of the city. The bloody confrontation nearly brought down the king.[22]

The uprising was ultimately suppressed, and the king retracted the promises he had been forced to make to appease the mob when it appeared to have the upper hand. However, with few farmers to cultivate the land, the peasants could easily flee and find better conditions elsewhere.[23] In fact, manorialism, the feudal system that bound peasants to a lord and his land, had already eroded in England by 1348, and much labor was already provided by negotiated contracts.[24] That meant a degree of freedom and of competition. It was the attempt by the lords to reimpose a stricter feudal system after 1348 that prompted discontent. Despite the failure of the revolt, the manorial system did not recover. England's population became less stratified.

Although the peasants did not seek to overthrow Richard II, the 1381 rebellion was revolutionary in that it created a model for mass resistance, something that had hardly existed before. Resistance to mask and vaccination mandates during the COVID-19 pandemic has provided a forum for mobilization and is also creating new models for mass resistance—street fights, truckers' convoys, armed protests and takeovers at state capitols, assaults on vaccination centers. The issues may fade, mass resistance may not.

The second takeaway is the recognition that the Black Death was not the sole cause of political turmoil in England. Changes in the climate, leading to extreme weather events, crop failures, and outbreaks of disease affecting domesticated animals, along with the heavy financial burden and cascading consequences of continuing war, combined to create a critical state of affairs and contributed to mounting social tensions. What happened in the distant decades of the fourteenth century is not that far from the situation we face today.

EUROPE'S CHOLERA RIOTS

We keep returning to the cholera outbreaks that repeatedly struck Europe during the nineteenth century. They are instructive for our inquiry. Although still different from our current environment, the situation in nineteenth-century Europe seems more akin to our current circumstances.

The cholera epidemics occurred during a politically turbulent time in Europe, marked by armed conflicts, social protest, sharpening political divisions, and a number of revolutions. Cholera added another layer of tensions. Political concerns and commercial interests in nineteenth-century Europe generally sought to deny, conceal, or diminish the existence of cholera, a behavior we have seen today. Efforts to control cholera in the nineteenth century sparked resistance, which frequently turned into riots. These riots occurred throughout Europe, from Great Britain to Eastern Europe and Russia, from cities in the north of Germany to Naples and Sicily in southern Italy. They numbered at least in the high hundreds. In the British Isles, the first wave of cholera, from 1831 to 1833, led to at least seventy-two cholera riots.[25]

Without benefit of the Internet or even evidence of communication among the rioters in various cities, common conspiracy theories motivated anger across the European continent.[26] Cholera hit the poor ruthlessly. The bacteria thrived in their crowded conditions, inadequate sanitation facilities, and—especially—contaminated water supplies, killing large numbers of those at the bottom of society. The unequal toll convinced many in the lower economic ranks that cholera was a deliberate plot by the elites to cull the poor and that government officials, doctors, pharmacists, and nurses were complicit in the planned mass murder.

The poison conspiracy was not equally embraced across Europe. It gained less of a foothold in Great Britain. Instead, members of the medical profession were suspected of killing off individuals to ensure a supply of cadavers for dissection.[27] The idea of a black market traffic in corpses had some basis in truth. Body snatchers, called "resurrectionists," were commissioned to illegally exhume bodies and deliver them to anatomy schools. In some cases, the body snatchers did not wait for a corpse but "burked" victims (suffocated them to leave little trace of violence) for their bodies.

Body-snatching rumors prompted several attacks on hospitals and medical personnel.[28] Cholera corpses significantly increased inventory, and the traffic in them reached an industrial scale in London.[29] Another conspiracy theory that affected nineteenth-century Britain asserted that, faced with overcrowding, authorities at mental institutions and hospitals, which also served as poorhouses, were "suffocating the poor" to be rid of them.[30]

There was a concurrent, albeit contradictory, rumor that cholera was a fiction designed to suppress the rights of the poor. The reality of dying people would seem to undermine this assertion, although notions of conspiracy and differing interpretations of reality, once adopted, can prove impervious to contrary fact. On the other hand, the harsh control measures—quarantines and *cordons sanitaires* that destroyed the incomes of workers, farmers, and petty merchants—that were applied unequally, coupled with the sometimes brutal response of the authorities to resistance, probably reinforced the view that the epidemics were being exploited to expand government control and suppress the rights of the economic underclass.

These nineteenth-century conspiracy theories marked a shift in popular attitudes. Evasion of and resistance to quarantines and other control measures date back centuries, but most of the popular aggression in the nineteenth century was directed against government authorities. As the power of the state to enforce control measures increased, people increasingly blamed the state itself, especially its administrative and medical bureaucracy.[31]

The later waves of cholera brought other issues. But the basic suspicion that the disease was created or exploited to kill off or suppress the rights of the poor persisted. These motives dictated targets that differed from those of the angry crowds in earlier pandemics. The rioters attacked medical personnel and hospitals, especially the facilities where cholera victims were segregated and which the rioters regarded as death chambers. In some cases, rioters managed to take over and briefly hold towns or neighborhoods. Generally, the cholera riots were local and short-lived, although in some cases they led to significant death and destruction. Over time, they became more violent, especially in Russia and southern Italy.

The nineteenth-century cholera riots coincided with labor agitation resulting from the terrible conditions created by the Industrial Revolution. According to many historians, however, the riots spawned by the epidemics did not cause or even precipitate the major political upheavals that swept across Europe in the early 1830s and again in 1848.[32] But the riots probably contributed to the continuing social and political tensions that manifested themselves in rebellions later in the century.[33] The cholera epidemics that struck Italy in the late nineteenth and early twentieth centuries, and measures by the government to control them, were complicated by the regional political divisions that persisted after the political reunification of Italy in 1870.[34]

The cholera riots intensified class hatreds. The rioters themselves were not revolutionaries and they presented no ideological or political program. This was not class warfare in the classic sense of a struggle over who would control the means of production—a contest of capital versus labor. Modern Marxist historians, however, have expanded the boundaries of revolutionary behavior to incorporate what they consider to be class-driven banditry or violent protests by the poor as a form of primitive or proto–class warfare.[35] As we discuss below, while not strictly revolutionary in the political sense, the discontents caused by the waves of cholera cannot be entirely isolated from the political struggles and growing tensions of the time.

In several respects, the dynamic of protests around the world during the COVID-19 pandemic resembles that seen during the cholera outbreaks. We have seen similar patterns of resistance, although fewer violent disturbances. Government is held accountable for failing to halt the spread of the disease, yet measures to control the contagion—and even administer a vaccine—are portrayed by some as tyranny. Political leaders and health authorities are the targets of popular wrath, with some receiving death threats and requiring personal security for themselves as well as their families.

The cholera epidemics of the nineteenth century also coincided with dramatic breakthroughs in understanding the source of the contagion, applying preventive measures, and creating an effective vaccine. In the first outbreaks, the concept of contagion based on the miasma theory that had originated during earlier epidemics still dominated. It was not until the latter part of the century that cholera was recognized as a waterborne bacterium—prevention required water treatment and sewage treatment systems. By the end of the century, a preventive vaccine for cholera had been developed—it was the first widely used vaccine made in a laboratory.

DEGENERATION

Attitudes toward epidemic outbreaks of disease in the nineteenth century—especially cholera but also the third wave of the plague at the end of the century—reflected social theories that were popular at the time. Social thinkers were increasingly obsessed with "degeneration," a fear that society was declining as a result of biological changes determined by habitat and heredity. Progress in the understanding of contagion and the role of sanitation was bringing about a fundamental transition from historical patterns of human suffering. The mass morbidity and mortality caused by infectious diseases, famine or poor nutrition, and backbreaking labor was gradually declining. Medical practice increasingly focused on individual disorders and the inevitable decline that comes with old age. Some in society, however, perceived a growing threat of "moral diseases."[36]

Degeneration theorists defined disease broadly to encompass medical and social pathologies. Maladies included not just physical ailments but mental deficiencies, immorality, and ideological disorders. Crowded living conditions, lack of sanitation, excessive consumption of alcohol, use of tobacco, lax morals, prostitution, sexual perversion, syphilis, physical weakness, laziness, insanity, feeble-mindedness, a propensity for crime, and susceptibility to contagious diseases—even to subversive ideologies like anarchism and communism—were all symptoms of a single pathology. According to the theory, the unequal suffering so apparent in the later epidemics of the nineteenth century was only partially the result of contemporary social inequities. It was believed to be inherent in the population affected.

Degeneration theory lent itself to racial theories of medicine. Other races had degenerated from the ideal physique and moral superiority of the white race. Indians, Chinese, and Africans were viewed not only as less civilized but as lesser beings.[37] The concept of a racial hierarchy carried over into a class hierarchy, with the lower classes in Europe's working districts and slums deemed to be lower on a presumed human scale—they were degenerates, culpable for their own dismal condition. Society was better off without them.

These notions were the basis for the racist theories that later characterized Nazi Germany, though they were expanded to other groups deemed "degenerate." Jews were defined as the lowest form of human and a threat to the superior Aryan race. Blacks, Slavic peoples, and Gypsies were also low on the hierarchy of races. Male homosexuals were to be eliminated because of their behavior, Jehovah's Witnesses because of their beliefs, Communists and Social Democrats because of their ideology. The physically and mentally disabled were the first to be systematically killed by the Nazis as they were unworthy of life and a threat to "race health."

Some of these attitudes did not entirely disappear in 1945 but remain relevant today, although in an altered form. While the initial numbers from the COVID-19 pandemic did not show Europe or the United States faring better than less economically developed countries (though in part this finding may be due to incomplete data), the limited availability of vaccines may in the long run result in even larger-scale outbreaks in Africa, South Asia, and Latin America. Travelers and refugees from these countries may be seen as an additional source of danger to be denied entry into the United States or Europe for reasons of national and health security. There is a racial component to this.

Blaming the victims for the cause of their suffering is already taking place in the United States. As we have seen, those lower on the economic scale have been hit harder by COVID-19. This reflects a host of factors, including fewer possibilities to flee, self-isolate, or work from home; more people living in multigenerational households; greater prevalence of preexisting health conditions such as obesity, diabetes, asthma, and heart disease, which increase mortality; and less access to quality health care. The unequal death tolls also reflect greater resistance to contagion control measures and vaccination in some communities. Even without considering the correlation between these factors and political attitudes, there is an overlap in the prevalence of the factors, which can be seen on a map. This has led to a different set of prejudices.

The continuing surges of COVID-19 in the United States affected the country unequally, with the fourth surge, caused by the Delta variant, and fifth surge, caused by the Omicron variant, affecting mainly—but not exclusively—the unvaccinated. This provoked growing intolerance and anger toward the unvaccinated, whose plight is seen as a consequence of their own behavior but also as a burden on all and a source of continuing danger to the rest of society. There is, however, a vast difference between blaming people who are vulnerable because they are less healthy and are more susceptible as a consequence of circumstances beyond their control, and holding individuals responsible when their continued vulnerability is a consequence of their own decisions.

THE 1918 PANDEMIC AND SOCIAL DISORDER

The second wave of the 1918 flu coincided with a revolution in Germany in November 1918, which reflected both the privations experienced during World War I and immediate postwar political tensions. The deaths caused by the disease may have added to the suffering caused by the war, and they certainly contributed to the dark atmosphere that prevailed in Germany during the 1920s. The connection between the 1918 flu and a general strike in Switzerland is clearer, as left-wing groups accused the government of responsibility for the toll of the disease on those serving in the army.[38]

The 1918 flu further highlighted the inequities in health care between colonial rulers and indigenous peoples, large numbers of whom had served in World War I. Anger over the high number of deaths and inadequacy of medical response contributed to protests and uprisings across the world, from Western Africa to New Zealand. The connection between the 1918 flu and the political instability that weakened Europe in the interwar years is more tenuous, although the third wave of the 1918 flu, in 1919, did adversely impact the Paris Peace Conference negotiations.[39]

For the most part, however, the 1918 flu did not arouse the race or class antagonisms that accompanied the epidemics of cholera and plague that occurred in the nineteenth and early twentieth centuries. "The disease [the 1918 flu] was too universal."[40] It killed all classes. The fact that the pandemic coincided with the final year of World War I may also have played a role. The patriotism brought about by the war engendered a sense of pulling together.

According to the Global Protest Tracker maintained by the Carnegie Endowment for International Peace, anti-government protests increased worldwide in 2020 and 2021. Most of the grievances in the early protests concerned racism, corruption, political oppression, or claims of fraudulent elections. Many of the later protests were directly related to the COVID-19 pandemic. Just as the 1918 flu cannot be blamed for the spread of the Bolshevik revolution or the rise of fascism in the 1920s, the COVID-19 pandemic did not cause the current surge in right-wing extremism, which began years earlier. However, the opportunity the virus offered to incite racism and exploit popular resistance to health measures has invigorated the extremists. A decline in infections and the relaxation of measures implemented to slow the contagion will remove those measures as a cause of protest, but it will not end the continuing economic hardships or protests against governments held responsible.

PANDEMIC COMMUNICATIONS

During the COVID-19 pandemic, public officials, especially at the federal level, were accused of providing inconsistent and sometimes conflicting information. This created confusion, cost credibility, and contributed to public anger and resistance to control measures and vaccination efforts.

Some of the inconsistencies were perhaps inevitable. The changing messages at the onset of the contagion reflected uncertainty at the time about the nature of the virus and precisely how it was spread—whether primarily by touching contaminated surfaces or by breathing contaminated air (and, if by air, what the ranges of safety were). Knowing nothing else, washing hands, disinfecting surfaces, social distancing, avoiding crowds, and wearing masks to reduce the spread of the virus through the air all made sense in dealing with any contagious disease.

As the virus continued to spread (then mutate) and medical professionals learned more, the recommended control measures were adjusted—usually to more restrictive rules. When it became clear that COVID-19 could not be stopped in its tracks and that its effects were often severe (especially among the elderly and those with other medical conditions), requiring weeks of intensive care, the major concern shifted to slowing the spread of the disease enough to prevent hospitals and health workers from being overwhelmed by the surge. But as economic and political damage mounted and resistance to controls increased, government officials also recognized the limits of both persuasion and regulation, and announced reductions even though these entailed risks. To critics, these changes and reversals seemed arbitrary and based on a political calculus, which to a degree they were.

It is essential during any crisis for those in charge to speak with a single voice, but that is always difficult in a nation as large and politically complicated as the United States. Governing a nation of 330 million people—especially cantankerous Americans—is challenging, and the U.S. system of separately elected governments at the federal, state, and local levels further complicates matters. Elected officials, from the White House to local school boards, are legally entitled to make their own decisions. Central command and unity of effort are hard to impose. President Trump famously claimed that he alone was in charge, but that was simply untrue.

Discord began at the top. President Trump gave marathon press conferences, often making incorrect or misleading assertions. He parted company with his most experienced medical advisors, publicly criticized them, then brought in others aligned with his views to contradict them. The news media were quick to amplify the differences.

COVID-19 spread during a contentious election year, guaranteeing that views of the virus would quickly be politicized, further adding to the divisions. Governors contradicted messages from the White House. County public health officials differed with their state governors. As a result, government—a plural entity—never spoke with a single voice, and an already divided public never listened as a single body but instead abided by what they chose to hear.

A credible and obvious voice of authority present at the beginning, Dr. Anthony Fauci, whose official title was director of the National Institute of Allergy and Infectious Diseases, was an excellent communicator. He was a man of science with vast experience in the field of contagious disease, a veteran of the HIV/AIDS pandemic, which, until the introduction of AZT in 1987, killed all of those infected. Fauci saw COVID-19 as a potential mass killer, and his paramount concern was saving lives. He spoke plainly—the pandemic was not good news. Tough measures were necessary to stop it, or at least slow it down. To do so, Fauci was even willing on occasion to correct a president who did not welcome dissent.

Although Fauci was an advisor with no inherent authority other than the power of persuasion, supported by his knowledge and personal conviction, never before had a single individual seemed to have the power to affect the personal behavior of so many people. Fauci became the face of government efforts to control the pandemic. While his plain speech helped to persuade millions of Americans to do their part, to go along with onerous rules to "flatten the curve," and to get the shot when a vaccine became available, it also made him a lightning rod for public frustration and pandemic fatigue. An increasingly ill-tempered audience saw him as a symbol of government oppression. In a stunning displacement of blame, people were angry at him for not stopping the pandemic; they were angry at him for the preventive measures he proposed; they were angry at him for dismissing un-proven cures, like hydroxychloroquine and ivermectin, that they thought would free them from both. Many de-spised him as a dangerous man. Some politicians said Fauci should be sent to jail. There were threats to his life, and since 2020, Dr. Fauci and his family have required personal security.

This trajectory says a lot about America at the time of the pandemic. Fauci was a man of science at a time when a growing number of Americans rejected science. That Fauci was clearly an expert in his field was a mark against him among those who distrusted experts, espe-cially medical experts. In the closed communities of those who rejected medicine—on religious grounds, or in line with political loyalties, or as members of in-groups like anti-vaxxers, those who simply hated all authority, or subscribers to conspiracy theories—medical experts like Fauci represented the enemy. They were evil.

The challenge of communicating across cultural boundaries reminded me of a crisis faced many years ago by a major American corporation whose founder was accused of worshipping the devil and devoting a share of the corporate profits to a satanic cult. This was one of those absurd urban legends or damaging market-place rumors that emerge from time to time. The narra-tive started with the typical claim: "A friend of a friend of mine told me that she heard so-and-so on *The Oprah Winfrey Show* (or some other popular talk show) admit-ting that she was a satanist and shared her profits with devil-worshippers." It is invariably "a friend of a friend" who saw the show—always impossible to track down.

Rumors, like viruses, spread quickly. Despite responsible public denials by the talk show hosts that no such interview ever took place, the rumor was off and running. Ingenious observers added to its momentum, declaring that the company's logo contained secret signs of the devil, or asserting that by taking the sixth letter of every sixth line on alternate pages of the company's annual report (or something like that) one could spell "Beelzebub," an alternative name for Satan. These fantasies had real effect. Customers at department stores hissed at sales clerks where the "satanic" products were sold. Graffiti appeared, along with petty acts of vandalism. Sales fell. The investigative company where I worked was called in to assist.

This was a different sort of investigation. There was no one person of interest. The rumor itself was our subject. The first task was to figure out where the rumor started and how it was spreading—a sort of epidemiological analysis. Looking at the date and location of every report of the rumor from sales outlets across the country, we were able to identify that the first documented case appeared in Pigeon Forge, Tennessee. From there, the rumor traveled along interstate highways east, south, and west—but, intriguingly, not north.

On a large map of the country, it looked like one of the spreading wildfires we are so accustomed to in the western United States. It enabled us to track where the rumor might turn up next. We needed to get ahead of the rumor—but how could we knock it down or at least create the equivalent of a firebreak to contain it?

Official denials were having no effect. The rumor continued to spread. Why? Who would believe such a thing? I consulted with psychologists, who told me a great deal about the dynamics of gossip and the spread of rumors. On a hunch, I also spoke to pastors. To believe in a rumor about the devil, they told me, one has to believe in the devil not as a theological abstraction but as a real being who tempts people to sin. Further inquiries led to the hypothesis that Christian fundamentalists had what modern medical researchers might refer to as the "preexisting conditions"—in this case, the beliefs—that made them susceptible to the rumor, which they were then likely to share with other like-minded individuals.

Using census data on religious affiliations, we were able to identify counties where there was a high percentage of potential believers. When we superimposed those on the map of where the rumor had already spread, we found a better than 90 percent overlap. That gave us a pretty good idea of where the rumor would continue to find tinder and enabled us to lay out where to create our firebreak. The question was how.

To belittle anyone's religious convictions was not going to be productive. It would not work to argue that belief in the devil was ridiculous. Instead, we thought that recruiting influencers—a term hardly used at the time—to talk to their followers would be a better approach. It was hardly a new idea. In wartime psychological operations, credible communicators are key.

We had to get out and talk to fundamentalist pastors who had large congregations and radio and television evangelists with big audiences, and explain to them how the rumor was doing harm—hurting people's jobs and causing great distress to the company's founder, who was in fact a devout Christian. We were ready to offer supporting information—such as the statement from the talk show's hosts—but at no time did we ever challenge the notion of the devil or disparage anyone's beliefs.

To convey this message, we identified and enlisted emissaries, those who would approach the influencers. Often, our recruits turned out to be respected members of the business community or former law enforcement officers—above all, people who lived in the same communities, spoke with the same accents, and frequently belonged to the same or neighboring congregations. The conversations were low-key, not sales pitches. We offered no scripts, no talking points. No one was pressured to sign on. The offer of material rewards would have been insulting. Those who listened were left to decide for themselves if they wanted to do anything. Most of them proved enormously helpful, even giving sermons against harmful gossip and rumors in general, and this one in particular.

As a result, the devil-worshipping rumor died down, although it never disappeared entirely and occasionally returns. As we anticipated, when it hit the firebreak, it mutated from devil worship to racism, found a new audience, and went on, albeit in a less virulent form.

I am far less confident that our early-1990s strategy would have worked in today's environment of twenty-four seven news channels, the Internet, and social media, or the deep political divides that punish any deviation from a narrow orthodoxy. The dismissal of science, the replacement of truth with assertions based on "alternative facts," the rejection of expert knowledge, and the impossibility of dismissing wacky conspiracy theories describes not just public affairs during the pandemic but Plato's "ship of fools."[41]

The ship of fools is an allegory for an anarchic and violent democracy where every individual is convinced that they possess knowledge and skills equal to all others, and therefore they need not listen to any authority or heed any advice to inform their decisions. It is a republic that denigrates wisdom. Instead, we are warned by the ancient philosopher, "the loudest voices will dominate, irrational, ill-motivated decisions will be made and the complex arena of politics . . . will turn into a crazy circus."[42] And it will end in tyranny.

Plato's *Republic* was written about twenty-four hundred years ago and reflected the sad fate of Athenian democracy, which no doubt motivated his harsh attitude toward the masses. We can argue about how to interpret Plato and his relevance to current events—contemporary philosophers have continued to do so for centuries. But one has to accept that the pandemic revealed attitudes and behaviors that raise questions about America's ability to address future national and global challenges.

CHAPTER 5:
EPIDEMICS AND
ARMED CONFLICT

POLITICAL PROTESTS LIKE those seen in 2021 in South America and Europe are common accompaniments to epidemics, as are increases in brigandage, banditry, and organized crime. Social unrest may turn violent. Government weakness and loss of legitimacy invite further challenges to state authority, which could escalate into local rebellions. Fragile governments may fall. All that, we have seen before. But do epidemics cause wars?

Throughout history, epidemics and wars have circled each other like binary stars. The great numbered plague pandemics of history actually encompassed hundreds of years of repeated outbreaks. The first plague pandemic began with the Plague of Justinian in 541–549 but also included successive epidemics of the bubonic plague that continued in the Middle East and Europe until 750. There were at least eleven separate outbreaks, some lasting several years.

The second pandemic, or Black Death, began in Europe

in 1347, with the first wave lasting until 1351. The pandemic coincided with the opening phases of the Hundred Years' War (1337–1453), which devastated the land—especially France, which was at that time the richest and most populous kingdom in Europe. "The countryside was pillaged, towns were sacked and burned, transport and communications were at an end, and prosperity and security vanished . . . brigands appeared everywhere,"[1] the art historian Joan Evans described. War caused this depredation; the plague contributed to the misery.

Bubonic plague became endemic and returned in successive waves until the late eighteenth century, with more localized outbreaks occurring somewhere in Europe almost every year between 1347 and 1671. It continued into the eighteenth and nineteenth centuries, with major outbreaks in 1710, 1738, 1743, 1770, 1772, 1812, and 1813. England in the fifteenth century had no less than twenty plague epidemics. London had forty major outbreaks in three hundred years, but the disease reappeared on almost an annual basis.

The third plague pandemic started in China in the late nineteenth century and continued for several decades. Between epidemics of the plague, there were seven global cholera pandemics beginning in the early nineteenth century and continuing into the twentieth century. Major outbreaks of typhus have occurred since ancient times—the Plague of Athens was probably typhus. Until smallpox was eradicated in 1980, epidemics of the disease occurred regularly. Europeans brought it and other contagious diseases to the Americas, where in a hundred years the new microbes wiped out as much as 90 to 95 percent of the indigenous people, who had no immunity to them.[2]

Major European kingdoms as well as local noblemen were almost continuously at war from the Middle Ages to the eighteenth century. The Italian wars, which started in 1494, lasted more than six decades. Fighting between Christian and Muslim rulers in Spain was almost constant from the eighth century until the end of the fifteenth century, and continued in the Mediterranean for several more centuries. The religious wars in France and Germany lasted 130 years. The wars for Dutch independence from Spain lasted eighty years.

Armed conflict was incessant. Armed rebellions, civil wars, and conflicts between nations are an almost constant feature of history. Global pandemics, with millions of deaths, occur more rarely, but local epidemics, some resulting in mass deaths, have been a regular occurrence. War, famine, and pestilence ride side by side. Epidemics were never far from wars, and wars were never more than a few years away from an epidemic. It is tempting to look for causality and deceptively easy to see it.

But caution is in order before we argue that the epidemics produced the turmoil. *Correlation is not causality.* History shows that armies spread diseases and wars have caused epidemics. And while outbreaks of disease have decimated armies, crippled military campaigns, and in some instances ended wars, showing that outbreaks of disease started wars is more complicated—there are no obvious straight lines from epidemic to armed conflict. Nor should we expect the same sequence of events to lead to the same consequences in every case.

The distinguished medieval historian Samuel Cohn convincingly shows that the Black Death was followed by a surge of local revolts affecting both northern and southern Europe, and that at least some of those revolts replaced specific group grievances with broader political rhetoric. But Cohn also warns that

> pinning long-term effects on single events is hazardous in any case and more so with such factors as levels of violence, difficult to quantify or judge qualitatively over a landscape as vast as Western Europe. The Black Death and its recurrences cannot be shown to have ushered in unequivocally a more 'violent tenor of life' that supposedly ensued over the late fourteenth and fifteenth centuries. Instead, stability, not violence, followed in some places.[3]

The consequences of the Black Death were not the same everywhere. But overall, the depopulation caused by the plague undermined the feudal system, clearing the way for the remarkable flowering of science and culture that came to be known as the Renaissance.

Cohn's cautionary advice carries even more weight as we attempt to examine the consequences of a pandemic, not just in one country or even on one continent but across the globe. It is also perilous to compare the Black Death, which killed 30 to 50 percent of Europe's population, with the COVID-19 pandemic, which, even in the hardest-hit countries, has killed no more than a few tenths of 1 percent of the population.

WHY PEOPLE TAKE UP ARMS

For decades, researchers have attempted to understand why people engage in political violence—riots, rebellions, terrorist campaigns, insurgencies, or civil wars. More than a half century ago, James C. Davies argued that violent upheavals were the consequence of "rising expectations." Revolution is likely when a sharp downturn occurs after a long period of rising expectations satisfied by material progress. Expectations continue to rise but they are no longer being fulfilled, creating a widening gap between elements of society that ultimately leads to anger and rebellion.[4]

In *Why Men Rebel*, Ted Gurr, one of the earliest researchers into the causes of insurgencies, advanced the theory of relative deprivation. He argued that the frustration-aggression theory developed by psychologists could be applied to societies as well as individuals.

Frustration leads to aggression, he noted, but not always. People may accept grinding poverty, starvation, and death from disease as the natural order of things. What pushes a society toward collective violence, according to Gurr's hypothesis, is the discrepancy between what people are getting and what they think they deserve.[5] Deprivation implies more than mere inequality. It suggests that an unequal and unfair system is depriving one portion of the population of what they need and deserve.

Both the rising-expectations and relative-deprivation theories could be applied to post-pandemic prospects for violence. As noted earlier in this study, absolute poverty has been steadily reduced in the world. The COVID-19 pandemic now threatens to reverse that trajectory, pushing more than a hundred million people into absolute poverty, including perhaps some who only recently were able to climb out of that status. This would theoretically create a worldwide condition of rising expectations dashed by disease. Whether and where such political upheavals may occur depends on local circumstances.

Since epidemics expose inequalities in society, they would also seem to fulfill Gurr's theory of relative deprivation. Because of unequal access to quality health care and different economic circumstances, many who may have felt they had an equal right to protection against a disease and against the consequent hardships caused by the contagion suffered more and will continue to suffer longer than others. Epidemics contribute to conditions that can lead to revolution and rebellion, which is not to say that they always do.

RECENT EPIDEMICS AND POLITICAL VIOLENCE

Neither Davies nor Gurr looked specifically at epidemics as a cause of rebellion; however, more recent research has explored the links between disease and political violence. Looking at wars between 1946 and 2004, Kenneth Letendre and his coauthors found that "in countries with high intensity of infectious disease stress, cultures are characterized by ethnocentric and xenophobic values" and that countries reflecting these values experience greater intrastate armed conflict and civil war.[6] This finding suggests that epidemics theoretically contribute to tendencies that correlate with internal armed conflict.

Celina Menzel examined the impact of infectious disease outbreaks on political stability by correlating the case numbers of Ebola, tuberculosis, and influenza with the level of political stability, defined by the absence of politically motivated violence according to an index es-

tablished by the World Bank. The index includes 131 countries and compares "the perceptions of the likelihood that
a government will be destabilized or overthrown by un-
constitutional or violent means, including politically
motivated violence and terrorism." However, it appears
that high levels of violence alone affect those perceptions.

In 2020, Singapore was listed in the index as the politically most stable country in the world, followed by New
Zealand, Brunei, Luxembourg, and Japan. (Owing to political turmoil and violence, the United States has since
2016 wobbled between twenty-fifth and thirty-eighth
place, even though the likelihood of the government being overthrown is low.) At the bottom of the list were Yemen, seen as the politically most unstable country in the
world, followed by Lebanon, Nigeria, Mali, and Zimba-
bwe. (Afghanistan, Syria, Iraq, Libya, and Somalia—all
war zones—are not included in the index.)[7]

Menzel's analysis concluded that, unsurprisingly, tuberculosis, which is chronically present and medically
familiar, has little effect on stability, while influenza has
a statistically significant but negligibly small effect. It
should be noted that these are correlations and not evidence of causality.[8]

Ebola, contrary to expectations at the beginning of the
2014–2016 outbreak in West Africa, did result in violence,
according to Washington University professor, Remi Jedwab, and his coauthors' research, but, according to Menzel, it did not contribute to instability.[9] Instead, it appears
to have had a long-term stabilizing effect. This finding
seems surprising in light of the fact that the governments
of the three African countries most affected by Ebola—
Guinea, Liberia, and Sierra Leone—deployed the military

to enforce strict lockdowns, quarantines, curfews, and checkpoints. In Liberia, soldiers took everybody with a high temperature into custody and searched for unreported patients, whom they brought to treatment centers guarded by the military. These measures provoked violent reactions, but the rapid decline in the contagion apparently quelled continuing resistance.[10] Compared with the civil wars and military coups that characterized politics in the three countries in the 1990s and early 2000s, political stability has improved, reflecting a trend not permanently reversed by the Ebola outbreak.

In *The Health of Nations*, Andrew Price-Smith updated William McNeill's observation in *Plagues and Peoples* that major outbreaks of infectious disease weaken state capacity.[11] To Price-Smith, this was a matter of increasing concern, as new pathogens were emerging and old diseases like tuberculosis and malaria were reemerging in more virulent forms. These diseases had devastating economic and social effects, especially on low-income economies, which in turn, Price-Smith believed, would have negative effects on political stability and would potentially threaten regional and global security.

That epidemics can worsen poverty is widely accepted and, as we have noted, this certainly appears to be the case with the COVID-19 pandemic. However, Price-Smith's arguments asserting a connection between epidemics and armed conflict within and between countries were seen as more dubious. Reviewers suggested that the analysis had too readily slid from correlation to causality, ignoring other factors, in addition to health crises, that were at work.[12]

Countries hit hard by epidemics, his critics suggested,

may also suffer higher levels of political violence, but that does not always mean that the epidemics are the cause.

In his more recent work *Contagion and Chaos*, Price-Smith argues that "pathogens can act as stressors on societies, economies, and institutions of governance. The proliferation of infectious disease may thereby compromise state capacity, and may destabilize the institutional architecture of the state."[13] However, he makes a distinction between a destabilizing effect and war, concluding that "epidemics and pandemics of emerging or reemerging infectious diseases may promote economic and political discord among countries, but are *unlikely* [italics added] to generate serious armed conflict."

Matteo Cervellati and his coauthors compared the "disease environment" and prevalence of civil conflicts between 1964 and 2004 in 140 countries. Their analysis showed that a "larger disease richness"—that is, the presence of multihost vector-transmitted diseases—was a "statistically robust and quantitatively relevant determinant of civil conflict."[14] Simply put, "countries with a high and persistent exposure to potentially deadly infectious diseases face a higher risk of violent civil conflicts."[15]

To counter the argument that the presence of disease is merely another attribute of economic underdevelopment and that, therefore, other factors, such as poverty and political fragility, might explain the higher levels of political violence, Cervellati and his colleagues were selective about the less-developed countries they sampled. They focused on non-OECD countries, thereby excluding the economically most advanced countries of the world, and on African countries, which are generally less developed. In both cases, the findings indicated that the presence of contagious diseases, and not just different levels of development, determined the prevalence of conflict.

It could be argued—as Stewart Patrick has done—that it is the prevalence of armed conflict that prevents public health systems from reducing disease. Patrick notes that "rampant disease is believed to further weaken already fragile states, depleting human capital, intensifying poverty, and in some cases exacerbating insecurity."[16] Furthermore: "Weak and failing states that descend into warfare typically experience a drastic reduction in health care delivery in conflict-affected zones, with a concomitant rise in infectious diseases." Hence, health workers flee to safer areas, clinics close down, travel becomes dangerous, funding does not exist. Unable to suppress contagious diseases on their own territory, these nations pose a threat to regional and world health security.

The Democratic Republic of the Congo, Iraq, and Syria are countries in which wars have seriously disrupted public health care. In some cases, the disruptions are deliberate. Rival armies have prevented food and medical supplies from reaching their opponents. The Syrian government stands accused of targeting hospitals and health facilities, along with infrastructure and food production, in areas not under its control, as part of its strategy to make life unbearable in rebel zones. In Pakistan and Afghanistan, guerrilla forces murdered health workers and deliberately prevented access to immunization against polio and other diseases.

In a recent study, Katariina Mustasilta warns that the COVID-19 pandemic will make bad situations worse in countries like Yemen, Libya, Ukraine, Sudan, and Colombia. For instance, in Yemen, Ukraine, and Colombia the virus contributed to the continuation of conflict, while in Libya and Sudan political violence escalated within months of the first identified COVID-19 cases.[17] The disease itself further burdens already stressed populations: in Yemen, 110,000 cholera cases, in addition to COVID-19, had been recorded by 2020. As of late 2021, more than half of Yemen's population faced acute food insecurity.[18]

Local and external conflict parties capitalize on opportunities to weaponize the pandemic to advance or consolidate their positions. The economic fallout further weakens already fragile government institutions. Food, medical relief, and vaccination efforts must navigate through a kaleidoscope of front lines and blockades of the increasingly fragmented security environments of local warlords, rebels, guerrillas, and bandits.[19]

In their recent article "After the Calamity: Unexpected Effects of Epidemics on War," Lazar Berman and Jennifer Tischler argue that "disease weakens states and their ability to project military power."[20] They also argue, however, that epidemics have spurred stricken societies to military action, making them more aggressive in the short term. Among others, they cite several historical examples, beginning with the Athenian Plague in 430 B.C.E., which broke out in the second year of the Peloponnesian War. At the height of the outbreak, the Athenian leader, Pericles, sent a large military force to attack the enemies of Athens. This lifted the morale of the Athenians and mobilized Athenian military forces out of the plague-stricken city.

Other cases cited by the authors include the practice among the Iroquois nations to conduct "mourning raids" to replenish losses from smallpox. It is true that the Iroquois and other American Indian tribes raided other tribes and sometimes white settlements, but not just to replenish losses from smallpox. These raids were an established form of warfare by the Iroquois and other tribes to take captives to torture and kill, enslave, ransom, or adopt into the tribe.[21]

There are also historical examples of epidemics so weakening affected countries that they invited foreign invasion. The Antonine Plague thinned the ranks of the legions protecting the Roman Empire's frontiers, inviting incursions by the Parthians in the east and Germanic tribes in the north. After years of hard fighting, the invaders were ultimately pushed back.

Some historians argue that the sixth-century Justinian Plague, along with years of continuous warfare, reduced the manpower resources of the surviving Eastern Roman or Byzantine Empire, crippling its efforts to recapture Italy from the Visigoths. But a recent military history of late Rome argues that loss of manpower caused by the plague was not the primary reason for Rome's military difficulties. "Enemies of Rome were able to collect large armies when the Romans were not."[22]

The biggest problem was the failure of the Eastern Roman Empire to pay its troops or raise larger armies. The plague did impact the economy, but the lack of funding for the military reflected policy choices—specifically Justinian's spending on church-building and other civil construction projects—and massive corruption in the bureaucracy. Despite the financial constraints, Byzantine armies were still able to achieve an impressive degree of military success.

Subsequent waves of the plague and continuous warfare on its frontiers over the next two centuries weakened the Byzantine Empire's defenses. A number of historians date the end of classical antiquity to the Islamic invasions of the seventh century, which are seen as a direct consequence of the Justinian Plague.[23]

As already noted, European conquerors and settlers brought with them diseases that decimated America's indigenous populations, reducing their capacity to resist the invaders.[24] The Europeans did not come to America simply because they knew the indigenous people had no resistance to imported pathogens, although the diseases facilitated their conquest and European military commanders were aware of their utility. There are reports that the British army in the eighteenth century sent smallpox-infected blankets and handkerchiefs to the Indians around their forts. The practice apparently had official approval. Lord Jeffery Amherst, who commanded the British forces in North America during the latter part of the French and Indian War (1754–1763), asked in a letter to one of his officers, "Could it not be contrived to send the Small Pox among those disaffected tribes of Indians?" In another letter, to the British official in charge of the "Northern Indian Department," he referred to "measures to be taken as would bring about total extirpation of those Indian nations."[25]

The Manchurian Plague in 1910 and 1911 did not so weaken China that it invited foreign military invasion, but it made China more vulnerable to foreign powers, already intent on carving the country into zones of influence. They exploited the difficulties caused by the plague to advance their imperial ambitions and extract further concessions.[26]

In sum, historical accounts of earlier epidemics offer numerous examples of sudden, large-scale outbreaks of disease resulting in collective violence in the form of violent protests, armed mobs, and localized rebellions, most of which were short-lived. Recent attempts to apply quantitative research methods to more complete databases and indices confirm correlations between epidemics and political violence, but the evidence that outbreaks of disease directly cause large-scale armed conflict—insurrections, revolutions, or wars between states—is less convincing. Although the economic suffering, social tensions, and political consequences of major epidemics have long tails and may contribute to later upheavals, disentangling the effect of epidemics from other factors is difficult.

Sudden outbreaks of debilitating disease can affect the course and outcome of wars. They can theoretically encourage military adventures to exploit weak opponents. More frequently, they can sabotage military campaigns.

As sources of political instability and agents of disruptive change in an already turbulent world, large-scale outbreaks of contagious disease have become a global security concern. They may push already fragile states into the "failed" category. They limit the ability of other nations to prevent human catastrophe. They impede the flow of aid to prevent starvation or public health assistance to limit further outbreaks of disease that may threaten the entire world. They increase human suffering and may generate refugee flows, which can lead to domestic and international crises. These effects may become visible only over longer periods of time.

As we have seen in our historical examples, war and disease often accompany one another. The coincidence of the COVID-19 pandemic and Russia's invasion of Ukraine is not without precedent. From Russian President Putin's initial decision to invade Ukraine to the effects of the pandemic on the course of the war and its consequences for COVID-19 (and other contagions), pestilence and war continue to gallop side by side.

Some Western analysts attribute Putin's decision to invade Ukraine at least partially to the two years he spent in extreme isolation as a consequence of the COVID-19 pandemic. During that time, he communicated with Russian government officials only by video conference. Many of the foreign dignitaries who came to Moscow to meet him also had to settle for video conferences, or submit to tests for the virus, or spend up to two weeks in quarantine. Even when granted an in-person audience, visitors had to pass through disinfectant tunnels and sit at the opposite end of a twenty-foot-long table.[27]

Putin spent much of this time in self-isolation elaborating his thoughts on Russia's rightful place in the world and its historical grievances against the West. A blend of historicism, mysticism, and messianic ambition, his analyses have an obsessional quality, as did his public comments.[28] Self-isolation facilitates self-radicalization. In Putin's case, the absence of normal personal interactions that might challenge his views was compounded by his absolute authority. Tyrants, who exercise supreme power over all aspects of life in their domains, often fall victim to the delusion that they are supermen—demigods—whose will has no limits. Surrounded by servile sycophants, their assessments are not questioned. There are no councils of war to raise different points of view. It can lead to dangerous miscalculations.

Statistically, Ukraine and Russia are close in the number of reported COVID-19 cases and deaths compared to their total populations, both residing in the top 15 percent of countries ranked in terms of deaths per million. Both countries have low overall vaccination rates, although by March 2022 Russia claimed to have done better, with roughly half of its population fully vaccinated as opposed to 36 percent in Ukraine.[29] Soldiers in both countries were almost entirely vaccinated.

Military analysts believe that pandemic disruptions adversely affected Russia's capabilities in a variety of ways. Lockdowns impeded military training, especially large-scale maneuvers. The pandemic's slowing of the global economy also led to a dramatic decline in the price of oil, which Russia heavily depends on for revenue, further reducing funds available for training. Russian pilots reportedly spent very few hours in the cockpit. Unconfirmed reports indicate that Russian officers were owed back pay. The Russian army was diverted to assist in the pandemic, building new treatment facilities and performing other forms of domestic assistance, which made sense in the medical emergency but further impeded readiness for a major invasion. Owing in part to COVID-19, military depots and repair centers operated at reduced capacity. Military equipment remained idle for long periods, causing further problems.[30] The effects of the pandemic would, of course, affect both countries, but the military demands were greater on the invaders than the defenders. And not everything can be blamed on COVID-19. Russia has a history of poor maintenance of its military equipment—corruption plays a large part.

Wars create ideal conditions for contagious diseases. Russia's invasion caused medical crises in Ukraine; its tactics were intended to do so. As in Syria, Russia resorted to military operations aimed at making life unbearable for civilians, deliberately shelling cities and targeting critical infrastructure, including health-care facilities. On March 22, 2022, Ukraine's Health Minister claimed that Russia had bombed or shelled 135 hospitals; the WHO confirmed 49 such attacks.[31] The strategy aimed at demoralizing the population and encouraging refugee flows that would upset Europe and reduce external support for Ukraine.

People living in cities under siege, without access to adequate food, drinking water, or sanitation facilities, are vulnerable to dysentery and other waterborne diseases like typhoid fever and cholera.[32] Ukraine's death toll from COVID-19, which already surpassed 100,000, may arc upward as access to medical care declines, oxygen supplies dwindle, and hospitals are overwhelmed by the wounded or destroyed by Russian attacks. The fog of war obscures accurate estimates. Nor do we know, in the spring of 2022, how this war will continue and what the consequences may be. But, with people in Ukraine dying from COVID-19 at the rate of eight hundred a day before the invasion, the pandemic—augmented by other communicable diseases that come with war—could turn out to be a bigger killer than the Russian army. In the largest movement of displaced persons in Europe since World War II, those fleeing Ukraine, crammed into packed trains and refugee centers, complicate pandemic control measures in European countries already facing rising case rates owing to a new Omicron subvariant.

The shape of the post-pandemic world, a term that—as of early spring 2022—must be used with extreme caution, will be determined by both the consequences of COVID-19 *and* the consequences of the war in Ukraine. It will be hard to disaggregate the long-term effects of the virus from the lasting aftereffects of the war, especially on the world's economy. The world will be seen as a more dangerous place, with greater risk than before. Isolation and national self-reliance will have greater value. Borders are back. But a more divided world may complicate cooperation against future pandemics and other global challenges.

CHAPTER 6: POST-PANDEMIC TERRORISM

FOR UNDERSTANDABLE REASONS, the connection between the COVID-19 pandemic and terrorism has become a subject of intense interest. Terrorism has commanded headlines for the past several decades, the pandemic for the past two years. Both are unseen enemies until they strike. Both contribute to a state of alarm, which some would argue is exaggerated. Both are perceived as direct threats to personal security. Both directly affect the daily lives of millions, from the removal of shoes before boarding airplanes to the mandatory wearing of masks. The efficacy of security measures taken to deal with both threats is challenged.

Fears of mass-casualty terrorism dramatically increased in 2001. The 9/11 attacks persuaded intelligence analysts and government officials that terrorist attacks of even greater magnitude were not only plausible but inevitable. The deadliest terrorist attacks in the 1970s had resulted in tens of fatalities. The totals escalated to hundreds of fatalities in the worst attacks of the 1980s.

In 2001, the death toll climbed to the thousands. These were orders-of-magnitude increases, leading many to imagine future terrorist attacks with tens of thousands or even hundreds of thousands of casualties. The only way death tolls of this scale could be achieved outside of conventional warfare would require the use of nuclear or biological weapons. The use of both became a presumption—"not if, but when," to use the popular phrase at the time.

The COVID-19 pandemic has caused deaths in the tens of thousands for many nations, in the hundreds of thousands for the hardest-hit countries, in the millions worldwide. Was the outbreak a natural occurrence? Was it the result of a leak from a laboratory? Or, as some have suspected, was it a deliberate act of bioterrorism?[1] The current investigation into whether the virus came from a laboratory in Wuhan, China, will keep suspicions alive. We should not expect the inquiry to yield "slam-dunk" conclusions; rather, there will be a range of explanations of the evidence available, with a range of probabilities. Mistrust will prevail.[2]

If the pandemic was not caused by terrorists or a hostile government, will it energize existing extremists or create new causes for future terrorist campaigns—anti-shutdown freedom fighters, anti-vaxxer armies? Will the pandemic inspire terrorists to adopt biological weapons?

WHAT HISTORY SUGGESTS

As we have seen, it is difficult to discern a direct link between past epidemics and armed conflict. It may be even more difficult to anticipate direct cause-and-effect links between the pandemic and terrorism. The pandemic is a global event with broad economic, social, and political consequences. Terrorism is an artificially defined subset of political violence. The pandemic has undoubtedly entered the mindset of extremists around the world. How it may influence the ways they incorporate it into their strategy and tactics remains to be seen.

History offers little guidance here. Epidemics have plagued the human race since the dawn of time. It is likely that some of the acts of violence that accompanied or followed the epidemics of antiquity and the Middle Ages would today be categorized as terrorism. The phenomenon of terrorism, as we currently understand the term, was not defined until the early nineteenth century.

Europe was an anxious continent in the nineteenth century. All of the European countries experienced political agitation, revolts, or civil wars. The second half of the century also saw the rise of anarchist violence, which the noted terrorism scholar David Rapoport has described as the first wave of modern terrorism.[3] Europe also saw six epidemic waves of cholera, which affected cities on the continent for more than eighty years between 1817 and 1899. Authorities saw both anarchism and "Asiatic cholera," as it was called then, as menaces coming from the poorer working classes.

As we have noted, many of the cholera epidemics that afflicted Europe in the nineteenth century caused violence, mainly in the form of riots in resistance to control measures and attacks on local public officials and health authorities. However, the pattern of the uprisings was "the product of local conditions . . . the rioters found no ideological point of departure to focus popular antagonism against the regime."[4] That seems very different from the situation in America today, where resistance to control measures followed and reinforced political polarity, although America's deep political divisions preceded the pandemic. That was also the case with the 1830 uprisings, which, in fact, preceded the cholera epidemic that struck Europe in 1831 and 1832. Similarly, the next major outbreak of cholera followed rather than preceded the second wave of revolutions in 1848. As Snowden notes, "Cholera moved in the wake of revolution rather than triggering it."[5] Misery drove the mobs. Epidemics made things worse but did not directly drive the political assassinations or anarchist bombings that came later.

More oblique connections, however, seem possible. European anarchists would, of course, have been aware of the epidemics and also aware of their unequal impact on the poor. A number of the noted revolutionary anarchists had firsthand experience. Pierre-Joseph Proudhon, who would become one of the intellectual founders of anarchism, saw his friend and financial supporter Gustave Fallot stricken and impoverished by cholera in 1832. (Fallot died a few years later.) Proudhon himself contracted cholera in 1854. Although the disease left him weakened for life, he survived, but his three-year-old daughter died of the disease. Johann Most, an ardent advocate of terrorist bombings, lost his mother, sister, and grandparents to cholera in Vienna in the 1854–1855 epidemic.[6] Errico Malatesta, a leading Italian anarchist, led a contingent of his revolutionary comrades to Naples to help the poor during the cholera epidemic of 1884. Several of the revolutionaries became infected and died.[7] The survivors later published a manifesto arguing that "the true cause of cholera is poverty, and the true medicine to prevent its return can be nothing less than social revolution." While some of these men were already opponents of established society when cholera struck, their personal losses fueled the fury and hardened the determination of a generation of violent revolutionaries.

As successive cholera epidemics continued during the nineteenth century, the spontaneous anger that erupted in cholera riots and political activism on behalf of an oppressed underclass perpetually beset by poverty, hunger, and disease coalesced into doctrines of revolutionary violence. This was especially true in the fifth cholera pandemic that struck Russia in 1891, where famine and accompanying disease may have killed as many as half a million people. The government managed the situation badly, initially failing to prevent the event or provide adequate relief and then reacting with harsh control measures that only increased the suffering. Fearing rebellion and an assault on the monarchy, the government of Alexander III, whose father had been assassinated and who himself had been the target of a foiled assassination plot, cracked down hard on possible sources of sedition. Tensions increased.

Again, cholera epidemics did not cause terrorism; they contributed to the radicalization that created terrorists. Critics of the economic system and the power structures that upheld it could portray epidemics as simply another manifestation of state violence against the people. Governments repeatedly failed to protect people from poverty, hunger, or disease, and when epidemics occurred, governments imposed oppressive control measures that increased public suffering.

The deep social and political tensions of the century provided fertile ground for the promotion of radical ideologies, deep-rooted prejudices, and conspiracy theories. The cholera epidemics added to the anxiety and expanded the battlefield between proponents of class warfare and conservative elements that saw the masses as dangerous sources of filth, idleness, debauchery, and disease.

TERRORIST VIOLENCE WILL CONTINUE

The debates about cholera and controls reinforced the existing political divides of the nineteenth century.[8] This resonates with current experience, particularly in the United States, where existing social divides and political polarization have shaped and intensified disagreements about the threat posed by the coronavirus and the control measures imposed by the government. COVID-19, like just about everything else in the United States, has become another partisan issue. People on one side view the virus as a major threat and largely accept government-ordered preventive measures such as social distancing, shutdowns, and mask-wearing. Those on the other side view the risks as exaggerated, see government health mandates as tyranny, consider wearing masks as useless, and favor outlawing health mandates or deliberately flout the rules.

Political partisanship, more than any other factor—including urban versus rural, income, race, and age—has determined behavior. The differences in attitudes did not soften as the pandemic surged but instead strengthened over time and were codified in state and local executive orders and legislation. The differences in public attitudes and behavior have resulted in higher per capita infection and mortality rates in counties that ignored or defied preventive precautions.[9] The divide continues with the approach to vaccination and the implementation of a vaccine passport system.

What has this got to do with terrorism? The partisan differences in response to the pandemic have led not only to differences in behavior but also to altercations and, in some cases, deliberate provocative confrontations. At the extreme, they prompted threats of violence against public and health officials throughout the United States and federal officials claimed to have foiled a plot by political extremists to kidnap and murder the governors of Michigan and Virginia.[10] The four men charged certainly talked about kidnapping the governor; their attorneys claimed that it was just talk and no more. A jury found two of the four not guilty and was unable to reach a verdict on the other two.[11]

In April 2022, authorities in Germany arrested four individuals for involvement in what they described as a plot by far-right extremists to spark a civil war in the country over COVID-19 restrictions. The plot reportedly included the kidnapping of the German health minister and sabotaging utilities to cause a nationwide power outage. The four had connections to right-wing extremists and groups protesting COVID-19 restrictions.[12]

Mask mandates have led to both spontaneous and premeditated violence. Vaccination sites have been attacked by anti-vaxxers. Speaking at a "Freedom Rally" against mask mandates in Pennsylvania, one candidate for state office called for "strong men" to physically remove members of school boards, which had ordered students to wear masks.[13] At another contentious school board meeting in Tennessee, a health-care expert who testified at the meeting was warned, "We know who you are. You can leave freely, but we will find you."[14]

Egged on by hundreds of anti-vaccine websites with millions of followers, reinforced by Russian, Chinese, and Iranian disinformation operations and domestic extremists, anti-vaxxers have made vaccination centers the targets of vandalism in the United States and Europe.[15] Research by the RAND Corporation showed that Russian news sources promoted conspiracy theories suggesting that contact tracing to control the spread of the virus was actually a plot by Western governments to spy on citizens and control populations. Dr. Anthony Fauci and the philanthropist Bill Gates, who donated millions of dollars to COVID-19 research, were frequently mentioned in connection with the alleged plot.[16] The general narrative was that political and class elites were promoting fear and advancing schemes to make society more submissive. These themes reinforced the attitudes of Americans already suspicious of the pandemic and opposed to government control measures.

Some European intelligence services warned in early 2021 that Russia was "counting on the COVID-19 pandemic to weaken unity in the West which would help Moscow gain a more prominent role in international affairs and lead to 'declining Western influence on the global stage.'"[17] The intelligence report concluded that 2021 would see Russian "influence operations designed to create and deepen divides within and between Western societies."[18]

In California, a man drove his car into health workers at a vaccine site, injuring one.[19] In August 2021, the U.S.

Department of Homeland Security warned that COVID-19 restrictions and vaccination were being used as a rationale to support calls for violence.[20]

Given the history of public behavior in previous epidemics, resistance to masks and vaccination should have been anticipated, but the virulence of COVID-19 denial and resistance to masks and vaccination has run far beyond what could have been predicted. There were clues, however. No one likes being told what to do, especially Americans. The United States has a long history of armed rebellions against the federal government, mainly in opposition to taxes, and the Internal Revenue Service has often been the target of bombings.

While Americans expect government to protect them against new dangers, they are easily enraged by personal inconveniences. We have seen this repeatedly in responses to airport security. All readily agree that terrorists and their bombs must be kept off of commercial airliners, but security procedures that require passengers to put their hand luggage on conveyor belts to be x-rayed, take their laptops out, empty their pockets, take their shoes off, remove their metal jewelry, and—heaven forbid—be subjected to a physical pat down prompt howls of protest and accusations of tyranny.

Mandatory face masks were seen by many as an affront to civil liberties and the American Constitution. Immunization, long a required and routine procedure for infants and toddlers, turned into something else when adults were told to get the jab. Opposition was more widespread than complaints about evil transportation security officers. Not everybody flies. The vaccination effort sought universal compliance, which makes sense from a public health perspective, but appears tyrannical to many citizens.

Opposition to vaccination results from a variety of motivations. Before the COVID-19 pandemic, many anti-vaxxers were predominantly concerned about the potential side effects of vaccines, which they believed caused autism and other medical conditions.

They were joined by people whose religious convictions persuaded them to avoid medical interventions. These convictions have become more pronounced during the COVID-19 pandemic. Vaccination itself is viewed as evil—the mark of the beast that would prevent salvation.[21] Patients with these convictions who were informed that they were dying of COVID-19 rejected the diagnosis. Admitting the illness would be tantamount to their abandoning God—or being abandoned by God.

Finally, minorities, in particular African Americans, have a deep suspicion of white medicine. With ample historical precedents to draw from, they suspect genocidal plots. Some minorities, already concerned about what they view as incremental tyranny, have chosen to make their stand on masks, vaccines, and vaccination passports.

Although some of the tension and anger may diminish as the contagion subsides, the mask and vaccination wars will leave a lasting legacy that reinforces existing anger and defiance that will continue to affect society and its governing institutions.

THE FUTURE TRAJECTORY OF TERRORIST VIOLENCE

International terrorism in its contemporary form—kidnappings, hijackings, bombings, assassinations, and armed assaults by groups operating internationally—emerged in the late 1960s, owing to a confluence of political circumstances and technological developments that made terrorist tactics an attractive mode of conflict. But most of the tactics employed by modern terrorists had much earlier origins.

David Rapoport dates the beginning of his "four waves of modern terrorism" to 1880, when anarchists began a campaign of assassinations and bombings.[22] The word, however, entered the political lexicon at the beginning of the nineteenth century, when in 1800 Napoleon Bonaparte's minister of police, Joseph Fouché, ordered the roundup of the terrorists responsible for an attempt to assassinate Napoleon with a bomb. And the concept and tactics of terrorism came even earlier. The word "assassin" itself derives from the eleventh-century Islamic sect that, lacking conventional military power, advanced its interests through the selective murder of high-ranking officials.

Looking ahead to the post-pandemic era, it is probably safe to assume that political violence in the form of terrorist attacks will continue. Viewed from a long perspective, armed conflict in general has lessened.[23] While the 2018 National Defense Strategy of the United States focused on great-power competition,[24] wars between nations—especially between great powers—have become rare events. Intrastate conflicts—civil wars, insurgencies, guerrilla wars, terrorist campaigns—also decreased in frequency and magnitude until the early 2010s but then increased.[25]

Conflicts within states appear more likely than conflicts between states. Intrastate conflicts entail irregular warfare and are likely to involve the use of terrorist tactics. Moreover, it would be a mistake to assume that wars involving the world's great military powers—the United States, Russia, China, the NATO alliance—would be confined to conventional military operations. Future armed conflicts, even between superpowers, could involve not only conventional battles between national armies but also the employment of terrorist proxies and political influence operations aimed at fomenting uprisings and resistance movements in the enemy's territories.[26]

COVID-19 IN THE CURRENT THREAT MATRIX

Terrorism tends to be episodic, but the phenomenon will persist. The question is, how might its future trajectory be affected by the COVID-19 pandemic?

Those already at the extremist edge see opportunities in the pandemic, as active terrorist groups attempt to incorporate it into their own belief systems and exploit it to rally their base and attract new recruits.

Islamic State (IS) propagandists have told their followers that the pandemic is their ally—"one of Allah's soldiers" sent to punish the infidels. COVID-19 is seen to offer opportunities for advancing the struggle. The devout are told that they should seek action. Al-Qaeda has taken a different approach, telling its followers that the isolation imposed by the pandemic should be used as an opportunity to improve their knowledge of the Koran.

Both IS and al-Qaeda had altered their strategy before the pandemic struck. For many years, al-Qaeda has lacked a safe geographic base and operational capacity to centrally direct large-scale attacks in the West, although its affiliates, including al-Qaeda in the Arabian Peninsula (AQAP) and al-Shabaab, have not abandoned the idea of launching overseas attacks. Al-Qaeda has sought to survive organizationally mainly by embedding itself in ongoing insurgencies in Afghanistan, Syria, Yemen, Somalia, and other areas where fighting continues.

Following the loss of its territorial caliphate in Syria and Iraq, IS has continued the conflict as an underground insurgency and, like al-Qaeda, has also embedded itself in insurgent movements in Africa and Asia. Some of these movements had previously announced their affiliation with IS when it was in its ascendency, to gain attention and advantages over local rivals. These insurgencies continue, reflecting local causes. IS will try to radicalize them into its global jihadist enterprise.

Much of the continuing terrorist violence in Africa and Asia falls in the category of being a component of local insurgencies. Historically, that accounts for a large share of the world's terrorist violence, but it differs from the isolated acts of terrorism in Europe, North America, and other Western countries.

The withdrawal of U.S. military forces from Somalia in 2020 and Afghanistan in 2021, and of French forces from the Mali in 2022 may reduce pressure on the insurgencies in these areas. The withdrawals are understandable from strategic and political perspectives, but they involve risks. The Taliban quickly toppled the Western-backed government in Kabul, which could in turn give its al-Qaeda allies more operational latitude. Taliban allies in Pakistan have intensified their campaign. Jihadists have managed to expand their presence in the Sahel in Africa despite European and U.S. efforts to contain them.

The point here is not to predict what will happen in these contests but rather to suggest that the contests will continue. As Russian revolutionary Leon Trotsky reportedly once observed, "You may not be interested in war, but war is interested in you."[27] The fact that we may choose to withdraw does not mean that these conflicts end—and that contributes to a continuing terrorist threat.

Both al-Qaeda and IS exhort individuals abroad to carry out attacks. This reflects one of the fundamental changes we have seen in terrorist organizations in the past twenty years. Traditionally, terrorists were recruited into small underground groups after careful vetting to weed out possible infiltrators or unreliable members. The Internet and social media changed that, making it possible for groups to recruit individuals and inspire action anywhere in the world. Loss of operational capabilities and a hostile operating environment made long-distance recruitment a necessity.

Recruitment by exhortation involves little investment and entails no risks, since the recruits know nothing about the organization. If they carry out a terrorist attack, the organization recognizes their contribution to the cause, giving them a kind of *ex officio, ex post facto* membership. Such recruitment is a low-yield activity. The groups reach out to hundreds of thousands of potential supporters. A few of the supporters take action. Those actors have limited resources and utilize primitive tactics— shootings where guns are readily available, stabbings, and vehicle-ramming attacks—against easy targets. Although crude, these attacks can nevertheless be lethal.

In June 2016, a gunman proclaiming allegiance to IS killed forty-nine people at a nightclub in Orlando, Florida. The following month, another individual drove a truck into a crowd celebrating Bastille Day in Nice, France, killing eighty-six. He, too, claimed allegiance to IS. In 2009, a U.S. Army major, inspired by al-Qaeda, killed thirteen people and wounded thirty-one at Fort Hood in Texas.

Meanwhile, violent domestic extremists have assumed greater prominence in the threat matrix of the United States and Europe. Of the potential sources of future terrorist activity in the United States, far-right extremists are probably better organized, trained, and armed than far-left extremists or the homegrown jihadists who, although inspired by groups abroad, are isolated individual actors. But the far right is also wary of the vulnerabilities that come with organization. Fearing infiltration by government agents, right-wing extremists in the United States have generally followed a strategy of "leaderless resistance," a notion popularized in 1983 by Louis Beam, a former member of the Ku Klux Klan.[28]

At the same time, an individual contemplating violence may view existing extremist groups as unsafe environments in which to share violent ambitions. The groups are currently under intense law enforcement scrutiny and may be riddled with informants. Although much recent media attention has been focused on organizations such as the Proud Boys, Oath Keepers, Boogaloo Bois, and Three Percenters, the greater threat of terrorism in the United States is likely to come from self-radicalized lone actors or tiny conspiracies outside or on the fringes of the larger organizations.

Anarchists have been active in the United States since the late nineteenth century. They have carried out assassinations and bombings and are frequently involved in street violence. Always opportunistic, anarchists attach themselves to popular protest movements. During the COVID-19 pandemic, some anarchists have reportedly participated in mutual aid organizations—an idea embedded in anarchist philosophy—much like their predecessors during the nineteenth century cholera epidemic in Italy. These activities have provided opportunities to promote anarchist principles by demonstrating that government is failing to meet the needs of the people, while nongovernment organizations could do so.[29]

Anarchism is an ideological movement rather than an organization. Anarchists tend to be organizationally chaotic, almost by definition, with both peaceful and violent factions and frequent ideological disputes. The more militant factions have benefited from the recent tumult and deep political divisions in the United States. Anarchist involvement in the Antifa movement and Black Lives Matter protests across the country has undoubtedly expanded the anarchists' personal contacts. Persistent protests in places such as Portland, Oregon, and Seattle require a degree of organization, but there is no central national command or organization. Again, terrorist violence beyond the throwing of Molotov cocktails is more likely to come from individuals or tiny conspiracies than from twenty-first-century clones of the left-wing terrorist groups responsible for continuing campaigns of violence in the 1970s.

Jihadist ideologies, white-supremacist and far-right beliefs, and, at the other end of the spectrum, anarchist ideas are the major galaxies of thought from which terrorists have repeatedly emerged. Revolutionary Marxism appears to be a fading driver of violence. Jihadism, as a source of inspiration for violence outside of the Muslim world, is a relative newcomer.

Terrorist attacks may also arise from new pandemic-created grievances and causes. The pandemic and the economic distress it is causing could change the way people behave in a (seemingly) more hostile world, the way they view the legitimacy of government authority, and how they value life itself. Despair, deep-seated prejudices, and conspiracy theories about COVID-19 or alleged government plots may propel acts of violence. Seething resentments caused by personal losses or the unequal effects of the pandemic on racial minorities and the poor may not always find space in the existing assemblages of the far left or far right. We could see the emergence of new formations.

According to a 2021 survey of UN agencies and offices and relevant affiliates by the United Nations Counter Terrorism Committee Executive Directorate (CTED), 44 percent thought that COVID-19 had increased the threat of terrorism in their respective regions. Fifty-three percent of the respondents believed that pandemic-related socio-economic and political impacts of the pandemic will increase the threat of violent extremism in the future, and 72 percent thought that countering violent extremism had become more challenging as a result of the pandemic.[30]

Both the United States and Europe saw the rise of anarchist groups following the 2007–2008 financial crisis and the imposition of austerity programs that mainly affected those lower down on the economic scale, although there was no spike in anarchist terrorism. The European continent also has seen a rise in right-wing nationalism, largely in response to long-term demographic changes and the recent influx of immigrants and refugees from Africa, the Middle East, and Afghanistan. Muslims and refugees in general figure prominently as targets of right-wing terrorism in Europe. This has led to an increase in incidents of violence, although the numbers remain small. The COVID-19 pandemic has seen an increase in attacks on Asians, especially in America.

The economic consequences of the pandemic and continuing conflicts in Africa, the Middle East, Asia, and Latin America will drive people attempting to escape absolute poverty and wars to migrate at a time when the tolerance for more foreigners is low. These tensions, which have already fueled acts of violence against immigrants and refugees in Europe, virtually guarantee future acts of terrorism, either by groups or—more likely—by individuals.

In many ways, the pandemic has increased the potential population of lone extremists. It has created a psychologically unsettling environment that promotes anxiety and apocalyptic thinking and persuades some people to believe in crazy things, which may inspire violent behavior.

Deprived of daily routines and personal relationships, many people are disoriented, disillusioned, and isolated—creating a receptive audience for fringe ideas and extremist ideologies. These are the conditions that psychologists believe can accelerate radicalization, which is an individual process reflecting personal experiences and circumstances as much as socioeconomic determinants or political convictions.

Isolation also weakens the normal checks on individuals' radicalization. Relatives and close friends, not authorities, are the first to notice unhealthy changes in attitudes or behavior and the first to intercede to keep those exhibiting them from spiraling toward extremism. Isolation reduces that vital human contact and removes the human control rods.

The expression of terrorist violence most likely will follow current forms. While extremist groups exist and are important sources of propaganda and psychological reinforcement, terrorism has increasingly atomized into individual behavior. Many of today's terrorists are self-selecting and organizationally untethered. They may be inspired as much by visions of death and destruction as by commitment to a specific ideology, which may serve only as a conveyor for their individual discontents. Many come with troubled personal histories of aggression, substance abuse, or mental problems.

The COVID-19 pandemic, in sum, has not seriously disrupted the ongoing jihadist campaigns in Africa, the Middle East, and Asia, nor has it muted the jihadist calls for terrorist attacks abroad. The pandemic does not appear to have reversed the rise of domestic violent extremism on either the far left or the far right—2020 and 2021 were tumultuous years in the United States and a number of countries in Europe, reflecting trends that preceded the pandemic. The pandemic has not reduced the deep political divisions in the United States, which reflect a decades-long trend. If anything, the pandemic has sharpened the divisions, which have determined the ways people have reacted to it and the measures taken to slow its spread.

The pandemic has added new motives for anger and potential terrorist violence—personal despair, the desire to blame someone—which often reflect deeply embedded prejudices and inspire new conspiracy theories. The social conditions imposed by the pandemic probably accelerated another already discernible trend toward individual action, motivated equally by personal circumstances. It is often difficult to distinguish politically motivated acts of terrorism from crimes motivated by hate or other acts of violence reflecting bizarre beliefs or mental instability.

At times, there have appeared to be two pandemics: the coronavirus, which immunization can ameliorate, and collective madness, for which there is no vaccine.

CHAPTER 7:
THE PANDEMIC AND
BIOTERRORISM

THE PLAGUE OF Athens is often cited as an ancient act of bioterrorism. Based on Thucydides' detailed observations about the symptoms, historians and medical specialists for many years have debated exactly what disease he was describing. Candidates include smallpox, typhus, typhoid, bubonic plague, measles, glanders (a disease that normally affects horses but can infect humans), and even ergotism—a condition that comes from eating grains infected by a particular fungus. Each theory has its backers and critics. Some argue that, under the desperate living conditions existing in a crowded city filled with refugees and under siege during war, its population could have suffered multiple diseases, which Thucydides conflated in his description.[1]

In a 2013 article, five researchers led by Manolis Papagrigorakis concluded that the pathogen—or at least one of the deadly pathogens—that killed so many Athenians was an earlier strain of typhoid, which was endemic at the time. The researchers point to Thucydides' description of the event and recent discoveries as corroborating evidence.[2] Specifically, they based this finding on an analysis of the DNA in the skeletal remains found in an ancient Athens cemetery dating to the period of the siege. Evolution of this pathogen over the centuries could account for the difference between the symptoms Thucydides observed and those indicative of the current form of the disease.

Thucydides also noted that the plague first attacked the population in Piraeus and from there spread throughout the upper city of Athens and beyond. Piraeus had no wells or running water supplies but depended on reservoirs, which could have been deliberately contaminated by Spartan saboteurs or sympathizers—as the Athenians suspected. Poisoning wells was not an uncommon tactic of warfare from ancient times into the twentieth century. The authors of the 2013 article are appropriately cautious in their conclusion, and their narrative is laced with hedging language like "would probably," "seems now more than ever possible," and "not difficult to imagine." It is, however, a reasonable explanation, although not likely to be the last word.

Ancient armies poisoned wells with the filth and carcasses of animals or with human corpses, knowing it would discourage their enemy from drinking the water or make them sick if they did.[3] They would not, however, have understood contagion in the way we do now. Until the late nineteenth century, the miasma theory—that disease was the result of noxious air rather than microscopic germs—prevailed. The discovery of germs led to a more scientific approach to biological warfare. Ancient and medieval armies could also have used what we would now call bioterrorism as a form of psychological warfare to create fear and destroy morale—for example, by hurling putrid corpses over the walls of cities under siege.

Parallel to today's pandemic and terrorism, anarchism and "Asiatic cholera" were the two great menaces of the late nineteenth century. Epidemics involving biological agents inspired the imagination of nineteenth-century novelists. In his 1895 short story "The Stolen Bacillus," H. G. Wells describes a plot in which anarchists plan to poison London's water supply with cholera bacilli.[4] Several other nineteenth-century novels also involve germ warfare. After the devastating effects of chemical weapons during World War I, biological warfare also seemed possible. The 1925 Geneva Protocol prohibited not only the use of poison weapons in war but also bacteriological methods of warfare.

The COVID-19 pandemic will no doubt give rise to a new wave of bioterrorism novels with a host of jihadist or domestic violent extremists playing the villains' roles. In this section, we ask the question, Does the pandemic increase the likelihood of bioterrorism?

The current pandemic does not offer terrorists or extremists new capabilities or point them toward a path they have not already thought about. The use of biological weapons in warfare has a long history, but actors outside of governments have entered the realm of bioterrorism on only a few occasions and generally have achieved little success.

In 1972, two college students in Chicago invented a terrorist group called the Order of the Rising Sun, or RISE, and plotted to contaminate the city's water supply with

Salmonella Typhi, which causes typhoid fever. The plotters, described as white supremacists, had acquired thirty to forty kilograms of typhoid bacteria cultures. Their objective was to wipe out the human race "except for a select group of people [who would be inoculated in advance and] who would live in harmony with nature."[5] The plot was interrupted by the FBI before any attempt was made.

In 1984, members of a religious cult in Oregon contaminated the salad bars of a town with *Salmonella* bacteria in order to incapacitate a portion of the populace during a local election where the cultists were trying to take control. More than seven hundred people were infected but none died.

In 1990, the Aum Shinrikyo sect in Japan, which later carried out a nerve gas attack on Tokyo's subway system, attempted to disseminate botulinum toxin, in the form of a mist sprayed from a moving vehicle, at two U.S. military bases, Narita Airport, the Japanese parliament, and the Imperial Palace. The effort failed to produce any significant results.

Aum Shinrikyo carried out six more biological attacks in 1993. In June, its operatives dispersed botulinum toxin in an attempt to infect guests at a royal wedding, again without results. The group then switched to using the anthrax bacillus for a second series of attacks in July. The first of these involved the dispersal of anthrax from a rooftop in Tokyo. The dispersal caused a foul odor but no documented cases of illness.[6] The group made several more attempts to disperse anthrax during the year.

In its final attempt, in 1995, Aum Shinrikyo planned to disperse botulinum toxin from spray devices concealed inside briefcases; however, the individual in charge had second thoughts and replaced the toxic solution with water.[7]

These attempts were part of a broader effort by Aum Shinrikyo to develop and use biological, chemical, and possibly even nuclear weapons. Like the Chicago plotters in 1972, whose objective was to start a new master race by killing off all others, Aum Shinrikyo's leader had visions of provoking a nuclear war that would wipe out the world's population. Only he and selected followers would survive to create a new race that would then repopulate the planet.

The theme of chosen survivors who rebuild humanity in a post-apocalyptic world figures in a number of terrorist plots involving weapons of mass destruction. Variations on the idea date back to Noah's Ark in the Hebrew Bible and the Hindu Dharmasastra and regularly recur in contemporary science fiction. As the noted American psychiatrist and author Robert Jay Lifton noted, "The quest for symbolic immortality is an aspect of being human."[8] These terrorist fantasies offer survival for the chosen and symbolic immortality for the superior race.

Al-Qaeda, which dedicates itself to mass murder, also attempted to weaponize biological agents, including anthrax, botulinum toxin, and ricin, and there are reports that it sought or acquired *Yersinia pestis* (plague) bacteria, the Ebola virus, and *Salmonella* bacteria.[9] These efforts failed. There were also a number of foiled terrorist plots and allegations of plots involving ricin in Europe, most recently in Germany in 2018. Although al-Qaeda's leaders were not thinking about rebuilding humanity, they felt entitled to kill millions of infidels in retaliation for their perceived aggression against Islam.

In 2001, a series of letters containing anthrax spores were mailed to news media outlets and Democratic senators in the United States, killing five people and infecting seventeen others as well as contaminating facilities that included a Senate office building. The arrival of the letters, which began a week after the 9/11 attacks, raised alarms that the United States now also faced terrorists armed with biological weapons and launched one of the FBI's largest investigations. A suspect was ultimately identified, but he killed himself before he could be arrested.[10]

All of the bioterrorist plots materialized in the closed universes of cults and mental disorder. The leader of the 1972 Chicago plot and the suspected author of the 2001 anthrax letters had both suffered mental problems. Apart from the very utilitarian aim of swinging a local election, the plotters' motives and ultimate objectives were unclear, grandiose, or bizarre. There is no proximity to previous pandemics or evidence that they provided any inspiration.

And, apart from the 2001 anthrax letters, most of the plots failed because of the difficulty of weaponizing biological agents and the technical limitations of the perpetrators. Even groups with manifest intentions, significant funding, and access to scientists, such as Aum Shinrikyo, which carried out the 1995 nerve gas attack on Tokyo's subways, were unable to successfully carry out a large-scale biological attack. However, technical limitations may not entirely explain the paucity of terrorist use of biological weapons. There also may be self-imposed constraints.

Jihadis may see the current pandemic as an ally, even though it has taken a heavy toll on Muslim nations. The virus has weakened or distracted security forces, and jihadi attacks have intensified in a number of countries during the pandemic. Jihad-inspired terrorist attacks have also occurred in Europe. But biological weapons, which kill the elderly, the infirm, and even young children, do not support the jihadis' image of themselves as warriors. Some terrorists may share the general revulsion that biological attacks provoke. Another factor that may dissuade terrorists from using biological agents is the reality that contagious diseases spread quickly and are indiscriminate in whom they kill. A group found responsible for a biological attack that spreads disease would quickly find itself reviled as an enemy of all humanity.

Notions of murdering millions appear to be most often associated with apocalyptic cults or religion-based and far-right ideologies. Bioterrorism scenarios, in particular, resonate with the genocidal fantasies of white-supremacist and anti-Semitic extremists. A poster circulated on the Internet advised followers, "What to Do if You Get Corona 19: Visit your local mosque, visit your local synagogue, spend the day on public transport, spend time in your local diverse neighborhood." This was more an expression of attitude than a terrorist plot.

However, several right-wing extremists in America were convicted of possessing plague, ricin, or botulinum toxin in the 1990s. The intended targets were not always clear, but most appear to have been government officials.[11]

Although most of the plots involving biological weapons were uncovered, and the attacks that resulted from those missed by the authorities resulted in deaths or illness on only two occasions (the 1984 Oregon incident and the 2001 anthrax letters), the fact that the current pandemic may be inspiring thousands more potential terrorists to even think about biological weapons is not a positive development. On the other hand, the COVID-19 pandemic may be prompting authorities to dust off forgotten plans for dealing with biological incidents, and that is a good thing. Large-scale biological attacks remain difficult to execute. Hoaxes and low-level attacks are far more likely and, given the anxieties already caused by the pandemic, they could cause great alarm.

The greatest danger comes from the possibility of state-backed projects. Conspiracy theories immediately linked the coronavirus to a Chinese government laboratory. Thus far, there is no concrete evidence supporting those theories, but the possibility exists that, under pressure of sanctions or during war, states or rogue elements within a state apparatus might consider the clandestine launching of a biological attack disguised as a natural outbreak.

The threat of a biological attack by a state is not new.[12] Both the United States and the United Kingdom considered the possibility of being attacked by biological weapons during World War II and the Cold War and prepared to respond in kind as a deterrent. The British program ended in the 1950s, the U.S. program in 1969.

Iraq under Saddam Hussein began developing biological weapons in the early 1980s. Mindful that Iraqi forces employed chemical weapons during the Iran-Iraq War (1980–1988), coalition forces sent to liberate Kuwait after its takeover by Iraq in 1990 were prepared for a biological attack, which never came. The full extent of Iraq's program became known after the Gulf War, and the program was considered to be largely dismantled by the late 1990s. However, allegations that Iraq was covertly continuing the effort were offered as one of the justifications for the U.S.-led invasion of the country in 2003. Post-invasion inspections showed that the biological weapons program had indeed been suspended.

The COVID-19 pandemic theoretically could inspire some countries to consider the utility of biological warfare. If the coronavirus becomes endemic, it theoretically could also provide cover for a covert operation. At the same time, however, the pandemic points to the risks that the virus might get out of control and harm the country that initiated an attack. In a post-pandemic environment, with hundreds of thousands already dead, the risks of retaliation would be extremely high, and affected nations might not wait for proof of culpability—suspicion of involvement might suffice.

Reflecting continuing concerns about al-Qaeda's interest in developing biological weapons, President Bush declared in 2002 that "the gravest danger to freedom lies at the perilous crossroads of radicalism and technology. When the spread of chemical and biological and nuclear weapons . . . occurs, even weak states and small groups could attain a catastrophic power." To prevent that from happening, the president warned, the United States would be prepared to take "preemptive action," including the use of military force.[13]

The declaration, which became known as the Bush Doctrine, was controversial, for it challenged the idea that military force could be used only in response to aggression, although the idea of preemptive action to prevent terrorists from acquiring or employing weapons of mass destruction had been around for decades. In principle, any government in possession of persuasive intelligence that a group or country was about to carry out a devastating attack on its population involving weapons of mass destruction might consider preemptive action rather than waiting for a devastating attack to occur.

As this brief review shows, the COVID-19 pandemic does not necessarily increase the likelihood of terrorists using biological weapons, although it may increase the appearance of such weapons in hoaxes, extortionate threats, and possibly low-level incidents. Calculations of the greater danger posed by state-sponsored attacks remain the same in a post-pandemic world as they were before the outbreak. Biological weapons are not reliable. They are indiscriminate. Contagious diseases, as opposed to toxins derived from plants or microorganisms, are difficult to control. And they entail high risks of massive retaliation and regime change.

CHAPTER 8:
LOOKING AHEAD

THE HISTORY OF past pandemics doesn't tell us exactly what the post-pandemic landscape will look like, simply that things will be different. Large-scale outbreaks of disease are often widely viewed as world-changing events. However, not all historians see even history's deadliest pandemics as drivers of dramatic changes; instead, some argue that the continuities exceed the disruptions.[1] This is an ongoing historical debate we are not going to resolve here.

Putting aside cataclysmic change, though, our survey shows that major epidemics have economic, social, psychological, and political effects that may persist for years, even decades. They carve a trail of lost lives, economic devastation, and personal despair. Epidemics expose and exacerbate existing economic inequalities. The poor become poorer. Political systems are turned upside down. Rulers fall. New forces emerge.

Epidemics leave legacies of distrust and disorder. They reveal and reinforce existing problems—poor governance, societal divisions, prejudices, inequality, corruption. Social and political cleavages intensify. They provoke unrest—anger, protests, civil disobedience, increases in violent crime. And although epidemics have seldom led directly to wars or revolutions, they can provoke social discord and political tensions, which in turn promote political violence.

Sometimes the effects of pandemics were observed during or soon after the upheaval. Others could only be discerned by historians writing decades, even centuries, after the events. In some cases, the consequences resulted from the epidemic itself; in others, from efforts to control it.

Many of the observed effects derive from a sort of *societal* comorbidity—the preexisting economic, social, and political conditions of a society. In the United States, a health emergency has come on top of a toxic political environment. The effects are complex, and it is difficult to disentangle the many possible contributors to the developments identified or to separate causality from correlation. Russia's invasion of Ukraine in the third year of the COVID-19 pandemic further complicates the post-pandemic landscape.

Comparing the effects of past epidemics with those of the COVID-19 pandemic begs the question: Is anything new? The same issues repeatedly emerge. Many of the effects observed in the current pandemic have been seen in previous large-scale outbreaks of disease. Then as now, political fortunes depended on how leaders handled a pandemic, something that is difficult to do well. Fairly or unfairly, political leaders are held responsible for the human suffering caused by the disease. Facing a contagion's inexorable spread, political leaders can only mitigate the consequences, not quell the disease. The rate at which people die may fluctuate, but the sum of deaths only increases.

Deeply divided constituencies guarantee that there will be political costs whatever course leaders decide on. Prioritizing commerce and personal choice can be perceived as denying, ignoring, or minimizing the deadly impact of the disease—a callous disregard for life. But imposing preventive control measures also comes at a political price. Draconian measures can be maintained only for short periods, not for months or years. COVID-19 already has produced political casualties. There will be more.

Scapegoating is a common feature of epidemics. Rulers may try to deflect public wrath by blaming foreign adversaries, domestic minorities, or recent immigrants. "Others"—whether Christians, Jews, Muslims, Hindus, Roma, Irish, Italians, Mexicans, Asians, and so on—have been blamed for the outbreak or spread of disease.

Our post-pandemic world will likely turn out to be a more turbulent and unpredictable place than pre-pandemic society. Wealthy islands will be surrounded by a sea of poverty worse than it was before. The economic damage wrought by the pandemic will take years to repair. The gap between rich and poor will grow even more. The world's poorest will increase in number, pushing migrant flows that provoke hostile reactions.

As of Spring 2022, Africa, Western Asia, and most of Latin America had not suffered the high percentages of deaths seen in Europe and the United States, although inadequate reporting may account for part of the disparity. If the virus continues to break out in new places or produces more contagious or deadlier versions that alter this picture, the flow of refugees from poverty, conflict, *and* disease will increase even further, adding to already high social tensions in destination countries. Again, the war in Ukraine, which in its first month already produced the largest number of refugees in Europe since World War II, further complicates the situation.

Europeans have shown greater sympathy for refugees fleeing Russia's brutal invasion of Ukraine than for those seeking to escape poverty and conflict in the Middle East and Africa. The absorption of Ukrainian refugees was also perceived as easier than the assimilation of those coming from less-developed countries. The sheer volume of Ukrainian refugees, however, could make European nations even less receptive to accepting other migrants, which will likely have economic and political consequences in the countries of origin.

Pandemics test the ability of societies to act collectively, either within nations or internationally. To do so effectively requires social capital—the notion of a community sharing values, norms, trust in institutions and each other, and a sense of shared purpose that is not imposed but freely agreed upon. It does not mean the absence of difference or debate but rather relationships that are marked by mutual respect and goodwill. That would hardly describe contemporary America—or indeed many countries today. Even countries such as Denmark and the Netherlands, which many would consider as rating high on a "social capital" index, have experienced violence in response to COVID-19 restrictions and requirements.

Had the COVID-19 pandemic posed a much greater threat to life, shared dread might have forced social bonding, although historically some of the deadliest outbreaks of disease led to some of most violent persecutions and bloodiest massacres, like those seen during the Black Death. The COVID-19 pandemic appeared serious enough to demand collective action but not dangerous enough to set aside our differences. We have the science to address the pandemic. We lacked the social accord.

In the United States, there was little social capital to begin with. The networks of filaments that connect Americans with each other have steadily dwindled. Americans do fewer things together, as witnessed by declining church attendance or membership in civic organizations and lodges. Parent Teacher Association (PTA) membership is a third of what it was in the 1960s. Traditional veterans organizations have struggled with declining membership. The shared national experience of military service itself ended with the end of conscription in 1973.

Modern communications—and especially social media—connect everybody but fragment them into quarreling factions. Mass media relentlessly excite their audiences with outrage—profiting from endless narratives of victims and villains. Contemporary politicians have learned how to design safe strongholds and win elections but they seem to have forgotten how to govern. Diversity is exalted by some, despised by others. The pandemic has not yet inspired the wave of terrorism that some fear, but recent public opinion polls in the United States indicate a greater acceptance of violence against the government.[2]

These trends began long before COVID-19, but the pandemic has accelerated the process. Social capital is about relationships. The pandemic severs them. It separates people, imposes social distancing, and enforces isolation. Post-pandemic society is likely to be more individualistic, more idiosyncratic in its beliefs. National consensus will be even harder to develop or maintain.

Epidemics challenge religious beliefs and religious institutions. Widespread death inevitably raises questions about individuals' belief in God. Some abandon their faith; others seek God's intervention through more fervent displays of devotion. Fanatics, false prophets, and religious cults arise. The COVID-19 pandemic and the resulting distress may change the way people behave in a seemingly more hostile world, the way they view the legitimacy of government authority, how they value life itself.

As the pandemic enters its third year, there is a growing sense of resignation that little more can be done. Some health officials are warning that, in the face of resistance to continuing preventive measures and vaccination, sooner or later everyone will be infected. Authorities can only hope to mitigate the medical consequences. Acceptance of that attitude underscores the limits of what government can achieve—perhaps a necessary recognition of the prevailing reality. But it also can be used to belittle future efforts to control major outbreaks of disease, which probably is the wrong lesson, going forward.

In his account of the Black Death, historian Francis Oakley noted that the plague not only spawned religious fanaticism and social unrest but promoted "the profound pessimism that is one of the distinguishing features of the later Middle Ages."[3] A series of unsettling blows to what was essentially a Christian civilization led to a shift in theological and philosophical thought "reflecting a catastrophic loss of confidence in the power and reach of human reason."

Although nowhere near the scale of mortality caused by the Black Death, the COVID-19 pandemic may also contribute to growing pessimism. Moodscapes are hard to track, but public opinion polling in recent years already points to a growing sense of malaise in many Western and some Asian nations. Whether the issue is the global economy; the national economic outlook or one's own economic future; the environment or personal health; or the dangers of war, terrorism, or crime—negative feelings, while wobbling from year to year, appear to have advanced.

America's disquietude preceded the virus, but the COVID-19 pandemic has spread a parallel epidemic of anxiety and anger. Events over the past thirty years have pummeled America's psyche. Rather than marking the "end of history," the end of the Cold War unleashed centrifugal forces, civil wars, ethnic conflicts, and global terrorist enterprises—a turbulent world in which technologically superior military power possessed by the United States offered fewer advantages. The 9/11 attacks demonstrated America's vulnerability to terrorism. It inspired fears of worse to come.

The 2007–2008 global financial crisis, the COVID-19 pandemic, current apprehension about whether the planet is doomed by global warming, and a renewed threat of nuclear war have all contributed to uncertainty about the future—about whether humankind even *has* a future. The anxiety and anger that preceded but have been intensified by the pandemic suggest a legacy of turmoil and strife that may not soon subside.

Johan Huizinga's description of European society after the Black Death as one in which people were "on edge, quick to violence" has ominous relevance today. Instead of a renewed sense of "we will get through this together," we seem to focus our attention exclusively on things that divide us. Public behavior has become coarser. There is a parallel pandemic of random aggression—automobiles deliberately driven into crowds, mass stabbings, acid attacks, people pushed off of subway platforms, fist fights on airlines. Violence against government is more acceptable.

Epidemics fuel rumors and promote conspiracy theories. They excite suspicions that sickness is being deliberately spread by foreign agents, subversive elements, or secret cabals. Conspiracy theories portray vaccination as a government plot to facilitate greater control over the population or as a genocidal scheme to kill off the poor or certain racial groups or political adversaries. With minor variations, these narratives have reappeared during the COVID-19 pandemic.

Yet, while many have wallowed in conspiracy theories, modern medicine has saved millions of lives. But we fail to honor the heroes. Public health officials are disparaged and threatened. There are no medals for those who fight or the many who have died on the front lines in hospitals; there is no recognition for those who invented the vaccines in record time.

A crude vaccination for smallpox was developed in the late eighteenth century. Vaccination against cholera became available near the end of the nineteenth century. There was no vaccine to save millions from death during the 1918 flu pandemic. A vaccine to prevent AIDS still eludes us. In contrast, effective vaccines were developed within a year of the first cases of COVID-19—an extraordinary achievement that has been met with unprecedented resistance (or misguided machismo), a fired-up anti-vaccination movement, suspicion of government and "Big Pharma," conspiracy theories, and—especially in America—political partisanship.

In public opinion polls taken before the pandemic, an overwhelming majority, including roughly the same number of Republicans (89 percent) and Democrats (87 percent) thought vaccines (referring to childhood inoculations for measles, mumps, and rubella) were safe.[4] Sixty percent of those responding to a 2015 poll who said they opposed vaccination described their political leaning as "liberal," but they didn't think their vote mattered much anyway. The pandemic has created dramatically more anti-vaxxers and changed their profile.

By March 2021, the percentage of Americans who said they opposed vaccination had grown from 9 percent in 2015 to 34 percent.[5] As the Delta surge swelled the numbers of those infected, this dropped back to 20 percent by the end of August 2021, which suggested that at least some of the opposition was more a reflection of hesitancy and changed with calculations of risk. But hard-core opponents of vaccination remained at 14 percent, still above the pre-pandemic figures.[6]

More intriguing was the politicization of attitudes toward vaccination. Whereas acceptance of vaccination had been bipartisan prior to the pandemic, vaccination increasingly became a political matter. Before the pandemic, Democrats were almost twice as likely—and Independents were twice as likely—as Republicans to say that vaccines were unsafe (9 percent of Democrats, 10 percent of Independents, 5 percent of Republicans).[7] As resistance to vaccination grew during the pandemic, anti-vaxxers became primarily Republicans.

It showed in the vaccination rates. By January 2022, 65 percent of the people living in counties that voted for Biden were fully vaccinated, compared to 52 percent of those living in counties that voted for Trump.[8] By the end of September 2021, 92 percent of Democrats were fully or partially vaccinated as opposed to 56 percent of Republicans.[9] Looking at it from the other direction: by October 2021, 17 percent of the unvaccinated were Democrats and 60 percent of the unvaccinated were Republicans.[10]

Public health policy issues had long been a political battleground in the United States, but never before had political loyalties so obviously determined individual decisions about health. It is a dramatic example of social identity dictating individual behavior. Group identity also has an enforcement effect. Anti-vaxxers are vocal in their opposition, boast of their refusal as a badge of honor, and urge others to resist, while those living among them who think otherwise remain silent, concealing their decision to avoid abuse. Some members of anti-vaxxer families secretly traveled to other towns to be vaccinated.

Political solidarity had measurable consequences. Data from December 2021 show that counties voting heavily for Trump had nearly three times the COVID-19 mortality rates of those that voted heavily for Biden.[11] Among the most fervent voters—that is, the tenth of the population living in counties recording the highest votes for Trump compared to the tenth of the population living in counties that recorded the highest votes for Biden—the reddest (pro-Trump) tenth suffered six times the ratio of deaths compared to the bluest (pro-Biden) tenth.[12]

Some readers may dismiss these statistics as fake news. Others may read them with Darwinian dismissal of those who make poor choices in life. I see the death of so many fellow Americans as a tragedy. The numbers are not small. One would have to compile the populations of all these counties to precisely calculate what the difference means in actual numbers but, even adjusting for heavily populated urban counties that voted Democratic versus less-populated rural counties that voted Republican, the difference could still come to tens of thousands of people—a significant and sad loss of life.

Far-right groups portrayed the mandates as another example of government tyranny, anti-vaxxers as an assault on bodily autonomy. Requirements to carry proof of vaccination to travel, enter certain premises, or work in certain professions prompted widespread protests. To those who already felt disparaged and besieged, vaccine passports raised the specter of yet another form of second-class status. Opponents quickly compared it to the phrase uttered by sneering, jackbooted officers in a hundred Hollywood films: "Your papers, please."

The overlap between right wingers and anti-vaxxers was evident in the early spring of 2020, when anti-vaxxers appeared in front of state capitols at armed protests opposing COVID-19 shut downs. A number of anti-vaxxers accompanied the mob that stormed the U.S. Capitol on January 6, 2021, in the attempt to overturn the 2020 presidential election results. Far-right extremists, including the Proud Boys (who were also involved in the

January 6 assault on the Capitol), participated in anti-vaccination marches.[13]

Similar protests occurred across Europe beginning in late 2021 and continuing into the new year. In January 2022, truckers opposed to Canada's vaccine mandates blocked bridges at the U.S.-Canadian border and converged on Ottawa, occupying the center of the city until police were able to regain control in late February. The Canadian truck drivers had a specific complaint—the requirement to prove that they were vaccinated when they crossed the border between the United States and Canada—but the protest became increasingly political and dominated by political extremists. Canadian flags on display were soon joined by flags of the American Confederacy, swastikas, and anti-Semitic slogans.

Extremist elements who comprised the core of the movement, motivated by conspiracy theories and anti-government and bigoted views, had been trying for years to organize a protest convoy but were unable to do so until the vaccine mandate gave them an issue with greater appeal and produced the reinforcements they needed.[14] Encouraged by political opponents of the Biden administration and right-wing media, a similar trucker-led convoy began circling Washington, D.C., in March 2022 to protest pandemic restrictions and vaccine mandates, even though those requirements had been lifted.

At first glance, a coalition of anti-vaxxers and far-right groups seems opportunistic and fragile, lacking any obvious unifying ideology other than a shared hostility toward government and political elites, a dismissal of scientific evidence, and fervent opposition to authority of any type. Stereotypical anti-vaxxers are supposed to be well-off yuppies and suburban moms who distrust pharmaceutical companies, favor homeopathic remedies, live in California, and shop at Whole Foods—unlikely allies of gun-toting white nationalists. The stereotype is obviously wrong. Polls conducted even before the pandemic showed that the average anti-vaxxer in America was a middle-aged, low-income, Midwestern male with a high school diploma, who was not necessarily a parent, lived in a rural area, didn't often go to doctors, and was less concerned about the environment—hardly a right-wing extremist, but far from the popular profile of anti-vaxxers.[15]

The alliance may lead to the emergence of a mutually beneficial and more permanent political movement. The far right is already an assemblage of groups with differing grievances and ideologies. Recruiting anti-vaxxers increases their political muscle and offers fertile ground for recruiting. At the same time, reinforcements from the far right increase the political reach and heft of the anti-vaxxers, although some in the movement might be uncomfortable with the beliefs of their new allies.

European countries also saw a coalescence of anti-vaxxers and far-right elements protesting vaccination mandates and passports. Even before the COVID-19 pandemic, people in some of the European countries had the lowest confidence in vaccines in the world. Percentages of Europeans opposing vaccination were on average twice those recorded in the United States (22 percent versus 11 percent according to a 2018 poll), with France reaching one-third who thought vaccines were unsafe. In the countries of the former Soviet Union, the percentages opposing mandatory vaccinations ranged even higher. Two-thirds of the people in Ukraine, possibly the most anti-vaxxer country in the world, did not trust vaccines.[16] As a result, Ukraine had one of the lowest vaccination rates in Europe.

Faced with widespread vaccine hesitancy, a number of European governments combined vaccine mandates with increasing restrictions targeting the unvaccinated. Those restrictions created a nascent underground where the die-hard unvaccinated led secret lives. Anti-vaxxers used counterfeit documents to prove vaccination for work or to gain access to restricted sites; they also created their own network of restaurants and other gathering places.[17] The long-term effects of this phenomenon are unclear, but protest movements tend to transform rather than retire. They aspire to become permanent parties. To maintain their tactical alliance, the far right and anti-vaxxers could find common ground on some issues that transcend the pandemic.

Opposition to all forms of compulsory immunization offers one issue where the two may come together. In America, political takeovers of local school boards, already a target of the far right for other reasons, could impede vaccination mandates or at least dilute their enforcement. The two movements conceivably could also unite to oppose science in general—a coalition of suspicious skeptics.

Or, the coalition of far right and anti-vaxxers could just be another example of how politics are being carved into thinner and thinner slices of zeal. In parliamentary systems, where the loss of a majority can mean the fall of the government, survival often depends on multiparty coalitions. Small movements holding just a few seats can become kingmakers. The same does not apply in America's presidential system, but any major, sustained national endeavor still depends on holding disparate groups together. Governing will be harder in the post-pandemic era.

COVID-19 could be a dry run for how we will respond to future dangers. What does the pandemic tell us about the ability of the world to address the challenges of climate change? It is already a contentious issue, with some claiming that global warming is a hoax being promoted for political or financial reasons. They see proposed guidelines aimed at reducing the use of fossil fuels, or restrictions on driving, as further examples of imminent tyranny. Others, worried about the future of the planet, are suggesting that violence is a justifiable course of action against countries or corporations that are unwilling to reduce activities that contribute to global warming. The philosophical arguments apparent in the response to COVID-19 will be replayed.

How will the COVID-19 pandemic end? It is not clear. The first wave of the "Spanish flu" began in the spring of 1918. After three waves washed across the world, it was essentially over by the summer of 1919. The 1957 Asian flu quickly spread from China to the rest of the world, but prompt vaccination ended that pandemic in 1958—although the virus continued to be transmitted at a low level until 1968, when it mutated into the Hong Kong flu, causing another pandemic. The Hong Kong flu pandemic affected some regions of the world until 1970 but then faded. (It continues to show up at low levels during annual flu seasons.)

By the spring of 2022, the world has experienced five waves of COVID-19. The fifth wave, driven by a new, more contagious variant of the coronavirus, which was first detected in southern Africa, prompted alarming headlines, border closures, and travel bans. A dramatic but temporary fall in financial markets underscored the precarious nature of the economic recovery. Investors anticipated a rapid and aggressive reaction by apprehensive governments, which would have adverse economic effects. The new variant—labeled Omicron—peaked quickly and turned out to be less lethal than initially feared, but the event underscored uncertainty about the future course of the pandemic.

The sighs of relief at the subsidence of the fifth wave turned out to be temporary. In March 2022, new-case numbers spiked to record levels in China and South Korea—countries that had escaped the ravages of the earlier waves. Cases were also coming back up in several European countries, creating fears that they would again rise in the United States. Officials worried whether the world was being engulfed by a sixth surge. The culprit was a new subvariant of the Omicron version, called BA.2, even more contagious than the original Omicron. The rising case numbers, however, coincided with widespread pandemic fatigue. While China and South Korea implemented tight controls, populations in Western countries resisted a return to lockdowns, limitations on gatherings, and especially a return to mask-wearing, despite the increased risk.

There would be no clear ending to the pandemic. Instead, COVID-19 may become endemic, with successive waves beginning in different parts of the world and quickly spreading, some more severe than others, prolonging uncertainty and hampering economic recovery. This is closer to the historical pattern of the Justinian Plague, the Black Death, and the repeated cholera outbreaks of the nineteenth century.

Projections of the pandemic's end—made before the Omicron variant was identified—pointed to rapid economic recovery in countries with advanced economies, which in fact seemed to be taking place, but suggested that developing countries with low vaccination rates would be affected by COVID-19 until 2023. Just months later, these projections seemed optimistic. The fifth wave and a possible sixth surge underscored the unpredictability of the virus, while the political and economic fallout of the war in Ukraine further complicated any predictions about the global economy.

While pharmaceutical and biotechnology companies appear adept at rapidly developing new vaccines to counter these mutations, the vaccines cannot be produced and distributed fast enough—or accepted by enough people—to knock out the virus worldwide, leaving large pools of unvaccinated people among whom new variants can emerge. This will impede global economic recovery and prolong economic hardship for many.

If a new, deadlier variant of the current virus or another pandemic-causing disease emerges years—or months—from now, will the experience of COVID-19 gained thus far enable the United States to handle it more effectively? Or will our social and political muscle memory take over to propel the country toward the same dysfunctional response?

The pandemic has tarnished America's reputation for

having the will, the resources, and the technical and organizational skills to lead ambitious global efforts. America led the effort to assist the world in recovering from the devastation of the Second World War, organizing a global economic, financial, and trading structure, building the coalitions and alliances necessary to protect the free world and prevent nuclear war and leading some of the most dramatic technological developments.

Despite the pronouncements by some, the world was never *America's* empire, nor did America own any century. America did see itself as exceptional and considered its values worthy of imitation, sometimes imposition. But a presumption of virtue can be an uncertain guide. The United States squandered opportunities and sometimes did harm, but it did have undeniable capacity and capability. These capabilities may have gradually eroded over the decades—or the problems became more intractable—but America still held on to a reputation.

The pandemic brought down the facade. The United States outpaced the world in total COVID-19 deaths, and the country's handling of the pandemic raised doubts about its credentials for leadership—at a time, tragically, when major global efforts are required to confront the dangers and meet the challenges faced by the planet. It is not just a matter of government competence. The pandemic has laid bare the flaws and fractures in American society. It will take a demonstrated determination and skill to recover.

Tension and anger may diminish as the contagion subsides, but the mask and vaccination wars will leave a legacy that reinforces existing animosity and defiance, which will continue to affect society and its governing institutions. Societies in many countries will remain divided domestically. Democracies will be harder to govern. Politics will increasingly be marked by defiance and intimidation. Terrorism will be seen by some as increasingly justifiable. Political coalitions will be harder to assemble and hold together. National efforts will be feebler. Extreme beliefs will prevail. The post-pandemic world may be filled with people seeking saviors—fertile ground for false prophets and dictators—or with nihilists who have abandoned hope and believe in nothing.

But there is a more hopeful scenario. The pandemic reminds us that the world is a dangerous place. Oceans provide no protection against disease. Greater self-reliance may be necessary, but no nation can isolate itself from the rest of the planet. We are in it together—survival requires a collaborative effort, perhaps more so now than ever.

The same lesson applies at home. The pandemic reminds us of our mortality. Those who read these words have survived—a reason for celebration, a cause for reflection. We are one nation, despite the efforts of cynical politicians, their media propagandists, and online rabble-rousers to divide us into little warring enclaves. They won't change, but we can. We, the people—not the demagogues, nor the would-be tyrants, nor the agitators, nor those claiming to be our saviors—*we* ultimately decide what kind of post-pandemic society we want to live in, what we want for ourselves, our children, and grandchildren. The pandemic hit us hard—more than a million dead in America alone, millions more made to suffer or mourn. The pandemic surely has changed every one of us. We can ensure that it is for the better.

DRAMATIS PESTILENTIAE

SCHOLARLY INTEREST IN the socioeconomic effects of epidemics has been growing, especially in the past twenty years. This brief guide lists the epidemics examined in this study that provided information about the immediate effects of epidemics on the economy and society and their longer-term consequences. It is by no means a complete chronology of epidemics recorded in history, which would include hundreds of entries.

The ancient Roman author Livy refers to epidemics occurring, on average, every eight years from 490 to 292 B.C.E. and every four years from 212 to 165 B.C.E.[1] Local outbreaks of the plague occurred frequently after the first major onslaught of the Black Death in the first half of the fourteenth century and continued into the late eighteenth century. Historians differ on the dates of the beginnings and ends of the subsequent outbreaks. Outbreaks of smallpox, cholera, yellow fever, typhus, typhoid, and other contagious diseases were almost annual occurrences for centuries.

430–426 B.C.E. PLAGUE OF ATHENS

There is no certainty about what the disease in this plague was, but it killed between a quarter and a third of the city's population. In response to the outbreak, Athens launched a military offensive against the Spartans, with whom Athens was locked in a bitter war. The Athenians at first blamed the Spartans for the outbreak but then turned on their own leaders. Thucydides observed that in reaction to widespread random death, people abandoned legal and moral constraints.

165–180 ANTONINE PLAGUE

Now believed to have been smallpox, the Antonine Plague was named for the Roman emperor Marcus Aurelius Antoninus Augustus, who ruled from 161 to 180. The plague killed 5 to 10 million people, perhaps 25 to 30 percent of the entire population of the Roman Empire.

249–275 PLAGUE OF CYPRIAN

Believed to have been an outbreak of hemorrhagic fever (although there are other possibilities), the Plague of Cyprian was named for Saint Cyprian, who witnessed and wrote about the outbreak. Between 5 and 10 million people may have died in this plague as it spread throughout the Mediterranean area. In some cities, it killed more than 60 percent of the population. Rome reportedly suffered 5,000 deaths daily. The plague depleted the Roman legions of manpower, inviting invasions on the empire's northern and eastern frontiers. There is evidence that towns well inside the empire hastily mobilized militias to man their own defenses against invaders and prevent anarchy.

541–549 JUSTINIAN PLAGUE

The Plague of Justinian was named for Emperor Justinian, who ruled the Byzantine Empire from 527 to 565. An outbreak of the bubonic plague, it is considered the first plague pandemic and it encompassed the entire Western world from Constantinople to the British Isles. Estimates of the death toll from this plague range between 30 and 100 million people, but historians accept that it killed half of the population of Europe.

558–749 SUBSEQUENT WAVES OF THE FIRST PLAGUE PANDEMIC

Bubonic plague became endemic in 558 and regularly reappeared in localized outbreaks over the next two centuries. Kyle Harper, in his intensively researched history *The Fate of Rome*, offers the most detailed catalog of the thirty-eight subsequent waves of the plague—or what he calls "amplification events."[2]

6TH CENTURY–1980 SMALLPOX

Descriptions of diseases with symptoms similar to those of smallpox suggest that the disease has been around for five thousand years. Some historians believe that smallpox was the disease responsible for the Antonine and Cyprian plagues. Smallpox is believed with greater confidence to have been responsible for outbreaks in Japan during the sixth century. A smallpox epidemic killed a million people in Japan from 735 to 737. Historians generally accept that the first smallpox epidemic in Europe occurred in 581. The most devastating outbreaks of smallpox occurred in the Americas. Imported from Europe in the early sixteenth century, during the next three hundred years smallpox (along with other contagious diseases against which the Native Americans had no immunities) would kill 50 to 60 million Native Americans, wiping out 90 to 95 percent of the indigenous population. Meanwhile, the disease continued to ravage populations in Asia, Africa, Australia, and Europe. During the twentieth century alone, smallpox was responsible for 300 to 500 million deaths and may have killed a total of a billion people before it was eradicated in 1980.

1347–1351 THE SECOND PLAGUE PANDEMIC, OR BLACK DEATH

The bubonic plague returned to Europe in the mid fourteenth century, when it killed between 25 and 50 million people (some historians put the total at 200 million), half or more of the continent's population. As in the Antonine and Justinian plagues, death on this scale meant widespread depopulation. In the United States today, it would mean losing 165 million people in less than the equivalent of one presidential term of office, and in Europe (not counting Russia), it would mean 350 million dead. The bubonic plague pandemics inspired dread, altered belief systems, collapsed economies, upended the social order, and overwhelmed political organization. Except for the annihilation of America's indigenous populations, the world has not witnessed mortality of this magnitude since.

1360–1773 SUBSEQUENT WAVES OF THE SECOND PANDEMIC

Further outbreaks of the bubonic plague occurred after 1360 and continued until the late eighteenth century. Combining various chronologies gives us a total of more than forty events—some more localized, some wider spread. This meant that, from the late 1350s to the early 1770s, outbreaks were occurring at an average of one every ten years. Since the outbreaks themselves often lasted several years, the plague was raging somewhere in Europe for nearly half of those four hundred years. During the same four centuries, Europe experienced hundreds of armed rebellions, civil wars, and major armed conflicts. Some of these wars continued for decades. Slaughter and contagion marched together across the landscape.

15TH CENTURY–20TH CENTURY
TYPHUS EPIDEMICS

Although there probably were outbreaks of typhus much earlier—an epidemic consistent with typhus was reported in the eleventh century, and typhus may even have been the source of the epidemic that devastated Athens in the fifth century B.C.E.—the first reliable descriptions come from Spain in the late fifteenth century. From then on, typhus epidemics were reported regularly. Spread by lice and closely associated with wars and other political upheavals, concentrations of troops, fleeing refugees, and prison populations, some of the outbreaks reached pandemic dimensions and had high death tolls. Between 1917 and 1921, there were an estimated 25 million cases of typhus in Russia, resulting in 2.5 million to 3 million deaths.

17TH CENTURY–20TH CENTURY
YELLOW FEVER EPIDEMICS

Yellow fever probably originated in Africa and was imported to the Americas as a consequence of the slave trade. Outbreaks frequently occurred in North and South America throughout the seventeenth, eighteenth, and nineteenth centuries, but only occasionally in Europe and not at all in Asia. The outbreaks were generally localized and, although deadly, never ascended to the level of pandemics. As many as 20,000 people may have died in a yellow fever epidemic that raged through the Mississippi River Valley in 1878. Yellow fever occasionally surges today, with deaths measured in the hundreds.

1817–1975 THE SEVEN MAJOR CHOLERA PANDEMICS

Cholera has been a common killer disease for centuries. Large-scale outbreaks still occur, often in war zones, although they do not attain the level of pandemics. Disease historians list seven major cholera pandemics:[3]

1817–1824 FIRST CHOLERA PANDEMIC

The first cholera pandemic began in India in 1817 and spread east along trade routes to Burma (now Myanmar) and Ceylon (now Sri Lanka). From there, it continued to spread through Southeast Asia, China, and Japan. At the same time, British soldiers brought it to the Persian Gulf, from which it spread to the Ottoman Empire and southern Russia.

1829–1837 SECOND CHOLERA PANDEMIC

This outbreak also began in India, and spread to Russia in 1831, where it killed 100,000 people. From there, it spread west through Europe. The pandemic reached the Americas in 1832, with major outbreaks along the St. Lawrence River in Canada and in the United States, Mexico, and Cuba.

1846–1860 THIRD CHOLERA PANDEMIC

Again, India was the source of this outbreak, which by the 1850s had spread to Europe, Africa, and the Americas. This was the deadliest cholera pandemic, causing deaths in the tens of thousands in many places. In Russia, it reportedly killed a million people.

1863–1875 FOURTH CHOLERA PANDEMIC

Muslim pilgrims carried cholera from India to the Middle East, and from there it spread throughout much of the world, benefiting from increased steamship travel. Port cities were particularly affected. Large-scale troop movements in Europe were another route of transmission.

1881–1896 FIFTH CHOLERA PANDEMIC

This wave of the disease, which killed about a million people, was not as bad as the earlier pandemics, as cities were beginning to improve their water supply and sewage systems, thereby eliminating a major reservoir for the disease.

1899–1923 SIXTH CHOLERA PANDEMIC

The effects of this wave were far less than those of earlier waves in most European cities, owing to a better understanding of germ theory and improvements in public sanitation. However, Russia suffered greatly, with a half million deaths, as did the Ottoman Empire and the Philippines.

1961–1975 SEVENTH CHOLERA PANDEMIC

A new strain of cholera appeared in Indonesia in 1961 and from there spread to India and the Soviet Union. There were smaller outbreaks elsewhere.

1855–1902 THIRD PLAGUE PANDEMIC

After a long hiatus, bubonic plague returned in the late nineteenth century. This outbreak began in Yunnan Province in China in 1855 and reached Hong Kong in 1894, India in 1896, and Madagascar and Japan in 1898. Further outbreaks occurred in Hawaii, Egypt, Europe, South America, and South Africa in 1899, and in San Francisco in 1900. Estimates of the total number of deaths range between 15 and 20 million worldwide, with 12 to 15 million in India alone. British control measures and medical practices caused deep resentment in India and Hong Kong. This pandemic also revealed racial and social inequities. In an effort to combat the contagion, Honolulu's Chinatown was entirely burned down, and harsh measures were imposed on the residents of San Francisco's Chinatown.

1889–1895 RUSSIAN FLU PANDEMIC

The Russian flu pandemic was caused by a new influenza virus (H1N1) first identified in Bukhara in 1889. It spread to the rest of Russia, reaching as far as Saint Petersburg. From there, it spread throughout the Baltic area, the Scandinavian countries, Germany, and on to France, Great Britain, Spain, and finally the United States. By

April 1890, outbreaks had been recorded in South America, Australia, New Zealand, and China. In all, the Russian flu (or "Asiatic flu," as it was also called) killed about a million people.

1910–1911 MANCHURIAN PLAGUE

The Manchurian plague was a pneumonic plague caused by a bacterium found in marmots, which were hunted in Mongolia and Siberia. This plague killed 60,000 people, far fewer than the hundreds of thousands who died in the cholera epidemics or the tens or hundreds of millions who died in the bubonic plague pandemics. However, it captured worldwide attention because of its "mysterious origin, rapid spread, and appalling virulence,"[4]—its death toll approached 100 percent. Japan and the European powers exploited the situation to advance their imperial ambitions in China.

1918–1919 THE 1918 (SO-CALLED "SPANISH") FLU PANDEMIC

This H1N1 influenza outbreak spread throughout the world and killed 50 to 100 million people in three years, making it the second deadliest plague in recorded history—although the population of the world in 1918, at 1.8 billion, was more than four times the population in the early fourteenth century, diluting its effects.

1957–1958 ASIAN FLU PANDEMIC

The H2N2 virus was first recorded in Singapore in 1957 and quickly spread to Hong Kong and then to the United States. The Asian flu reportedly killed 1.1 million people.

1968–1970 HONG KONG FLU PANDEMIC

The H3N2 virus was first detected in Hong Kong in 1968. It spread throughout Southeast Asia and then to the United States, the Panama Canal Zone, and the rest of the world. American soldiers returning from the war in Vietnam were one source of transmission, responsible for the cluster of cases in the Canal Zone. The Hong Kong flu was responsible for between 1 and 4 million deaths worldwide.

1981–PRESENT HIV/AIDS

The origins of the HIV/AIDS pandemic have been traced to Africa, but the disease quickly spread throughout the world. More than 77 million people have been infected with HIV, and 26 to 46 million have died. There is no vaccine or cure for the HIV infection, although treatment regimens have improved, saving lives.

2002–2004 SARS (SEVERE ACUTE RESPIRATORY SYNDROME) PANDEMIC

SARS is caused by a coronavirus, like COVID-19. The 2003 outbreak infected more than 8,000 people in twenty-nine countries, leaving almost 800 dead. Although the death toll was comparatively small, the nature of the disease and the rapidity of its spread caused worldwide alarm.

2009–2010 SWINE FLU PANDEMIC

Debate still rages as to whether this new strain of the H1N1 virus emerged from pigs in Mexico or China. It quickly spread throughout the world, killing between 150,000 and 575,000 people worldwide.

2012–PRESENT MERS (MIDDLE EAST RESPIRATORY SYNDROME)

Since 2012, twenty-seven countries have reported cases of the highly lethal MERS virus first found in Saudi Arabia. It is associated with infected camels, but human-to-human transmission is possible if the individuals are in close contact. Thus far, the virus has killed approximately 800 people.

2014–2016 EBOLA VIRUS PANDEMIC

The Ebola virus was identified in 1976 but surged in a pandemic that affected several West African nations in 2014. The virus killed approximately 10,000 people.

2019–PRESENT COVID-19 PANDEMIC

As of late April 2022, the COVID-19 virus infected more than 500 million people worldwide and killed more than 6 million, making it the deadliest outbreak of disease since the 1918 flu; however, its death toll has a long way to go to match that of the 1918 outbreak.

ACKNOWLEDGMENTS

I AM INDEBTED to all of the authors of the fascinating histories of previous epidemics whose books and articles I have quoted extensively. Their works should be mandatory reading for officials dealing with the COVID-19 and future pandemics. Their scholarship has inspired and guided this inquiry.

A book is a group project. I want to thank David Lubarsky for his constant encouragement, his continuing support, and his always helpful comments. Whatever I happen to be thinking about, Anita Szafran assists in helping me find often-obscure references. Janet DeLand has edited my writing for many years and continues to help me express my thoughts correctly and clearly—and, I hope, with some measure of grace. John Warren, a longtime friend and colleague, remains an ally in disseminating my views. I am grateful to Dennis Johnson for making Melville House the forum for publication and Carl Bromley for his thorough review of the manuscript and valuable substantive as well as additional editorial suggestions. Kyle Hoepner made the critical final copyedits.

Reading the histories of pandemics past is a sobering reminder of the catastrophes contagious disease can bring. I therefore want to express my admiration and appreciation of the public health officials, scientists, physicians, and frontline health workers who have valiantly endeavored to contain this latest outbreak of disease. They have protected so many of us, risked their own lives to save the lives of others, and created and delivered new vaccines and therapies—and, in return, they have too often been repaid with disregard, calumny, abuse, and threats. To each and every one of you, I thank you for your service to humankind.

ENDNOTES

AUTHOR'S NOTE

1   Nicolas Stockhammer (ed.), *Key Determinants of Transnational Terror-ism in the Era of COVID-19 and Beyond: Trajectory, Disruption, and the Way Forward*, Vol II, 2021.

INTRODUCTION

1   Patricia Brown, "The Role and Symbolism of the Dragon in Vernacu-lar Saints' Legends, 1200–1500," 1998. In a fascinating chapter, "Dis-ease, Dragons and Saints: The Management of Epidemics in the Dark Ages," in Terence Ranger and Paul Slack (eds.), *Epidemics and Ideas: Essays on the Historical Perception of Pestilence*, Cambridge Univer-sity Press, 1992, Peregrine Horden examines the persistence of the pestiferous dragon as an important concept that framed how people viewed and dealt with disease.

2   These include William Rosen, *Justinian's Flea: The First Great Plague and the End of the Roman Empire*, 2007. Numerous accounts and anal-yses of the Black Death that ravaged Europe in the fourteenth century include Norman Cantor, *In the Wake of the Plague: The Black Death and the World It Made*, 2001; David Herlihy, *The Black Death and the Trans-formation of the West*, 1997; and Rosemary Horrox (trans. and ed.), *The Black Death*, 1998. See also Laura Spinney, *Pale Rider: The Spanish Flu of 1918 and How It Changed the World*, 2018. Detailed local analyses are presented in Richard J. Evans, *Death in Hamburg: Society and Politics in the Cholera Years*, 1987; Roderick E. McGrew, *Russia and the Cholera: 1823–1832*, 1965; Steven Porter, *Black Death: A New History of the Bubon-ic Plagues of London*, 2018; and Frank M. Snowden, *Naples in the Time of Cholera: 1884–1911*, 1965. Broad historical surveys of epidemics include Samuel K. Cohn, Jr., *Epidemics: Hate and Compassion from the Plague of Athens to AIDS*, 2018; J. N. Hays, *The Burdens of Disease: Epidemics and Human Response in Western History*, 1998; Joshua S. Loomis, *Epidemics: The Impact of Germs and Their Power over Humanity*, 2018; William H. McNeill, *Plagues and Peoples*, 1976; and Frank M. Snowden, *Epidem-ics and Society: From the Black Death to the Present*, 2019. The books mentioned here, along with other scholarly works and press articles cited in the endnotes and the list of works consulted (see this book's website), are only a small part of the epidemic library.

3   Hans Zinsser, *Rats, Lice and History: A Chronicle of Pestilence and Plagues*, 1934, p. 128.

4   Ibid.

5   Jared Diamond, *Guns, Germs, and Steel: The Fates of Human Societies*, 1997, p. 197.

6   Snowden, *Epidemics and Society: From the Black Death to the Present*, op. cit., p. 2.

7   The 1918 flu pandemic came to be called the "Spanish flu" only be-cause censors in other countries blocked mention of disease outbreaks during World War I while Spain did not. Some now criticize use of the

term as offensive. Accordingly, it will be referred to here simply as the "1918 flu pandemic" except in cases where it is part of a direct quote. Matthew Brown, "Fact Check: Why is the 1918 flu influenza virus called 'Spanish flu'?" *USA Today*, March 23, 2020. Many histories of epidemics still use the term "Spanish flu." If all geographic adjectives for epidemics are considered to be in bad form, then future authors will have to consider renaming the 1957 "Asian flu," the 1968 "Hong Kong flu," MERS (Middle Eastern Respiratory Syndrome), and the Ebola virus named for the Ebola River in Africa, although, unlike the deliberately mislabeled "Spanish flu," these outbreaks were first identified in these locations.

8   Johns Hopkins, *Coronavirus Resource Center*, "COVID-19 Data in Motion," updated daily.

9   Britt Clennett and Karson Yiu, "China orders 51 million into lockdown as COVID surges," *ABC News*, March 14, 2022.

CHAPTER ONE: THE HUMAN TOLL

1   The estimate of 25 million deaths appears in "Outbreak: 10 of the Worst Pandemics in History," *MPH Online*, undated; the 30 million to 50 million estimate appears in Ker Than, "Two of Histories Deadliest Plagues Were Linked, with Implications for Another Outbreak," *Nationalgeographic.com*, January 31, 2014.

2   "Outbreak: 10 of the Worst Pandemics in History," op. cit.

3   The 15 million estimate appears in John Frith, "The History of the Plague—Part 1. The Three Great Pandemics," *JMVH (Journal of Military and Veteran's Health)*, Vol. 20, No. 2, undated.

4   Thucydides, *The History of the Peloponnesian War*, Book II, Chapter 7.

5   Gene A. Brucker, *Renaissance Florence*, 1969.

6   David Nirenberg, *Communities of Violence: Persecution of Minorities in the Middle Ages*, 1996.

7   Dave Roos, "Why the 1918 Flu Pandemic Never Really Ended: After Infecting Millions of People Worldwide, the 1918 Flu Strain Shifted—and Then Stuck Around," *history.com,* December 11, 2020.

8   Zinsser, op. cit., p. 299.

9   Joseph M. Conlon, *The Historical Impact of Epidemic Typhus*, 2007.

10   Lindsey Theis, "How Might COVID End?" *Newsy*, August 23, 2021.

11   Institute for Health Metrics and Evaluation, "Current projection scenario by April 1, 2022," *COVID-19 Projections*, updates regularly.

12   The estimates of war casualties derive from a number of sources, which often differ widely but fall within the ranges shown.

13   Vaclav Smil, "China's great famine: 40 years later," *BMJ*, December 18, 1999.

14   UNAIDS, "Global HIV & AIDS statistics—Fact sheet," updated periodically.

15   Bipin Dimri, "The Chinese Famines of 1907 and 1959: Natural Disasters or Man-Made?" *Historic Mysteries*, July 21, 2021.

16   David Adam, "The pandemic's true death toll: millions more than official counts," *Nature*, January 31, 2022.

17   Laura Santhanam, "COVID helped cause the biggest drop in U.S. life expectancy since WWII," *PBS Newshour*, December 22, 2021.

18   Andrew Noymer and Michel Garenne, "The 1918 Influenza Epidem-

ic's Effects on Sex Differentials in Mortality in the United States," *Population and Development Review,* Vol. 26, No. 3, 2000.

19 Marilynn Marchione, "US Life Expectancy Drops a Year in Pandemic, Most Since WWII," *AP News,* February 17, 2021.

20 Latoya Hill and Samantha Artiga, "COVID-9 Cases and Deaths by Race/Ethnicity: Current Data and Changes Over Time," *KFF,* February 22, 2022.

21 Worldometer, *Coronavirus Cases,* updated regularly.

22 Lauren Frayer, "India's Real Death Toll May Be Many Times Higher Than the Official Count," *NPR,* April 29, 2021.

23 National Center for Health Statistics, "COVID-19 Mortality Overview," updated regularly.

24 Andrew Stokes et al., "Assessing the Impact of the Covid-19 Pandemic on US. Mortality: A County-Level Analysis," *medRxiy,* September 25, 2020; see also Boston University School of Public Health, "US COVID Deaths May Be Undercounted by 36 Percent," undated.

25 Krutika Amin and Cynthia Cox, "COVID-19 Pandemic-Related Excess Mortality and Potential Years of Life Lost in the U.S. and Peer Countries," *LawFare,* April 13, 2020.

26 *The Economist,* "The pandemic's true death toll: Our daily estimate of excess deaths around the world," December 29, 2021.

27 Haidong Wang et al., "Estimating excess mortality due to the COVID-19 pandemic: a systematic analysis of COVID-19-related mortality, 2020-21," *The Lancet,* March 10, 2022.

28 Spinney, op. cit.

29 Lee Mordechai and Merle Eisenberg, "Rejecting Catastrophe: The Case of the Justinianic Plague," *Past & Present,* Vol. 244, Issue 1, August 2019.

30 Asa Briggs, "Cholera and Society in the Nineteenth Century," *Past & Present,* Vol. 19, Issue 1, April 1961.

31 Evans, *Death in Hamburg: Society and Politics in the Cholera Years,* op. cit.

32 Snowden, *Naples in the Time of Cholera, 1884-1911,* op. cit.

33 Alan Maryon-Davis, "Outbreaks Under Wraps: How Denials and Cover-Ups Spread Ebola, Sars, and Aids," *Index on Censorship,* March 12, 2015.

34 Nick Wadhams, Jennifer Jacobs, and Bloomberg, "China Intentionally Under-Reported Coronavirus Cases and Deaths, U.S. Intelligence Says," *Fortune,* April 1, 2020.

35 Sonia Shah, "Contagion in New York City: 1832," *DP,* November 10, 2014.

36 Marilyn Chase, *The Barbary Plague: The Black Death in Victorian San Francisco,* 2003, pp. 72–80.

37 Ed Mazza, "GOP Leader Who Fought Against Vaccine Dies After a Week-slong Battle With Coronavirus," *Huffpost,* August 20, 2021. The official who made the claims died of the coronavirus on August 19, 2021.

38 Allan Smith, "'I'm Looking for the Truth': States Face Criticism for COVID-19 Data Cover-ups," *NBC News,* May 25, 2020.

39 Geoffrey Parker, *Global Crisis: War, Climate Change & Catastrophe in the Seventeenth Century,* 2013, pp. 616–617.

CHAPTER TWO: DEEP ECONOMIC SCARS

1 Congressional Research Service, *Global Economic Effects of COVID-19,* updated December 10, 2021.

2 "U.S. economy plunges 31.4% in the second quarter but a big rebound is expected," *AP*, updated September 30, 2020.

3 Ayhan Kose and Naotaka Sugawara, "Understanding the Depth of the 2020 Global Recession in 5 Charts," *World Bank Blogs*, June 15, 2020.

4 Ibid.

5 Aaron O'Neill, "Global unemployment rate up to 2020," *Statista*, August 3, 2021.

6 International Labour Organization, "World Employment and Social Outlook Trends," June 2, 2021.

7 Jon Hilsenrath and Sarah Chaney Cambon, "Job Openings Are at Record Highs. Why Aren't Unemployed Americans Filling Them?" *Wall Street Journal*, July 9, 2021.

8 Oxfam International, "Ten richest men double their fortunes in pandemic while incomes of 99 percent of humanity fall," January 17, 2022.

9 "The Pandemic's Early Effects on Consumers and Communities," *Consumer & Community Context*, Board of Governors Federal Reserve System, p. 1, Vol. 2, No. 2, November 2020.

10 Elise Gould and Melat Kasas, "Young Workers Hit Hard by the COVID-19 Economy," October 14, 2020; United Nations International Labour Organization, "COVID-19 and the World of Work. Seventh Edition," *ILO Monitor*, January 25, 2021.

11 Ibid.; see also Chang Ma, John Rogers, and Sili Zhou, "Modern Pandemics: Recession and Recovery," August 2020.

12 Eli Rosenberg, "Hotel Industry Emerges from Pandemic with New Business Model, Possibly Fewer Workers," *The Washington Post*, June 11, 2021.

13 Indermit Gill and Phillip Schellekens, "COVID-19 Is a Developing Country Pandemic," May 27, 2021.

14 Fernand Braudel (ed.) *Villages désertés et histoire économique (XIe-XVIIIe siècle)*, 1965; Herlihy, op. cit.; Cantor, op. cit.; John Kelly, *The Great Mortality: An Intimate History of the Black Death, the Most Devastating Plague of All Time*, 2005.

15 Congressional Research Service, op. cit.

16 "Covid Could Push Over 200 Million More People into Extreme Poverty," NDTV, December 6, 2020.

17 The World Bank, *Global Economic Prospects*, June 2021.

18 International Monetary Fund Research Department, "Chapter 2: After-Effects of the Covid-19 Pandemic: Prospects for Medium-Term Economic Damage," *World Economic Outlook*, April 6, 2021.

19 Economist Intelligence Unit, "Q4 Global Forecast: One Year On: Vaccination Successes and Failures," November 2021.

20 Statista, "Share of Adults Who Are Fully Vaccinated Against COVID-19 in the European Economic Area (EEA) as of November 4, 2021, by Country."

21 Ibid.

22 Josh Holder, "Tracking Coronavirus Vaccinations Around the World," *The New York Times*, March 15, 2022.

23 Statista, "Share of Adults Who Are Fully Vaccinated," op. cit.; see also Stephen Paduano, "Is Africa Headed for a Financial Crisis?" *Foreign Policy*, August 10, 2021.

24 Maria Cheng and Farai Mutsaka, "Scientists Mystified, Wary, as Africa Avoids COVID Disaster," *AP News,* November 19, 2021.

25 Haidong Wang et al., "Estimating excess mortality due to the COVID-19 pandemic: a systematic analysis of COVID-19-related mortality, 2020-21," op. cit.

26 International Monetary Fund Research Department, "Chapter 1: Global Prospects and Policies," *World Economic Outlook,* April 6, 2021.

27 "Allianz: Companies Need to Prepare for More Political Disturbances and Violence Ahead," *Allianz Press Release,* March 24, 2021.

28 Douglas Irwin, "The Pandemic Adds Momentum to the Deglobalisation Trend," *VOXeu,* May 5, 2020.

29 Lexi Lonas, "Apple Says Supply Issues Cost Company $6 Billion in Fiscal Fourth Quarter," *The Hill,* October 29, 2021.

30 Gita Gopinath, "The Great Lockdown: Worst Economic Downturn Since the Great Depression," *IMFBlog,* April 14, 2020.

31 U.S. Bureau of Labor Statistics, *Employment Situation News Release,* March 4, 2022.

32 Joshua Freeman, "Pandemics Can Mean Strike Waves," *Jacobin,* April 7, 2020.

33 Charles P. Pierce, "Forget the Haircut Protesters. There's a Real Labor Movement Blossoming in America," *Esquire,* April 29, 2020.

34 Matthew Boesler, Joe Deaux, and Katia Dmitrieva, "Fattest Profits Since 1950 Debunk Wage-Inflation Story of CEOs," *Bloomberg,* November 30, 2021.

35 Peter Whoriskey, Douglas MacMillan, and Jonathan O'Connell, "'Doomed to fail': Why a $4 trillion bailout couldn't revive the American economy," *The Washington Post,* October 5, 2021.

36 Tom Spiggle, "What Does a Worker Want? What the Labor Shortage Really Tells Us," *Forbes,* July 8, 2021.

37 Aimee Picchi, "A Record 4.4 Million Americans Quit Their Jobs in September," *CBS News,* November 12, 2021.

38 "Why the Great Resignation is Happening in Europe Too," *YPULSE,* November 2, 2021.

39 David Dayen, "The Great Escape: Why Workers Are Quitting Their Jobs, After the Trauma of the Pandemic," *American Prospect,* November 29, 2021. Analysts have offered a variety of explanations for the increase in the number of voluntary departures.

40 OECD, "Wage Levels," *OECD Data,* updated regularly.

41 Paul Krugman, "Whatever Happened to the Great Resignation?" *The New York Times,* April 5, 2022.

42 World Economic Forum, *Global Risks Report 2022,* January 11, 2022.

CHAPTER THREE: EFFECTS ON SOCIETY

1   The vivid descriptions of life in the late fourteenth century are described in the first chapter, "The Violent Tenor of Life," in Johan Huizinga, *The Waning of the Middle Ages,* (Garden City, NY: Anchor Books, 1954). A more recent version is Johan Huizinga, *The Autumn of the Middle Ages,* (Chicago, IL: University of Chicago Press, 1996).

There are multiple translations of Huizinga's famous volume written in 1919, and therefore language varies.

2   Huizinga, op. cit.

3   Snowden, *Naples in the Time of Cholera, 1884-1911*, op. cit.

4   Snowden, *Epidemics and Society: From the Black Death to the Present*, op. cit., pp. 81–82.

5   Ibid.

6   Pere Salas-Vives and Joana-Maria Pujadas-Mora, "Cordons Sanitaires and the Rationalisation Process in Southern Europe (Nineteenth-Century Majorca)," *Medical History*, Vol. 62, No. 3, July 1962.

7   Adam Klein and Benjamin Wittes, "The Long History of Coercive Health Responses in American Law," *Lawfare*, April 13, 2020.

8   Snowden, *Naples in the Time of Cholera, 1884-1911*, p. 253.

9   Ranger and Slack (eds.), op. cit., p. 233.

10 Naomi Wolf, "US Becoming 'Totalitarian State' with COVID Lockdowns," *Newsmax*, February 23, 2021.

11 Catharine Arnold discusses mandatory mask wearing and resistance to the mandate in *Pandemic 1918: Eyewitness Accounts from the Greatest Medical Holocaust in Modern History*, 2018, pp. 164–168; see also Bruno J. Strasser and Thomas Schlish, "A History of the Medical Mask and the Rise of Throwaway Culture," *The Lancet*, May 22, 2020.

12 John M. Barry, *The Great Influenza: The Story of the Deadliest Pandemic in History*, 2005.

13 Richard Coker, "Are the British Conformist or Libertarian? Our Face Mask Response Is Telling," *The Guardian*, July 20, 2020.

14 Zacc Ritter and Megan Brenan, "New April Guidelines Boost Perceived Efficacy of Face Masks," Gallup, May 13, 2020.

15 Susan Page and Nada Hassanein, "No vaccination? Americans back tough rules and mask mandates to protect the common good," *USA Today*, August 22, 2021.

16 The College of Physicians of Philadelphia, *The History of Vaccines*, 2011.

17 Benjamin Franklin, "Preface to Dr. Heberden's Pamphlet on Innoculation, 16 February 1759," *Founders Online*, National Archives.

18 Robert M. Wolf and Lisa K. Sharp, "Antivaccinationists Past and Present," *BMJ*, August 24, 2002.

19 Peter Furtado, *Plague, Pestilence and Pandemic: Voice from History*, 2021, p. 208.

20 Kevin M. Malone and Alan R. Hinman, "Vaccination Mandates: The Public Health Imperative and Individual Rights," in Richard A. Goodman et al. (eds.), *Law in Public Health Practice*, 2006.

21 Furtado, op. cit., p. 301.

22 Giovanni Boccaccio, *The Decameron*, 2003.

23 Brucker, op. cit., quoting Boccaccio.

24 Centers for Disease Control and Prevention, *Risk for COVID-19 Infection, Hospitalization, and Death by Race/Ethnicity*, June 17, 2021, updated periodically.

25 Filipa Sá, "Socioeconomic Determinants of COVID-19 Infections and Mortality: Evidence from England and Wales," *VOXeu*, June 8, 2020.

26 Paulo Ricardo Martins-Filho et al., "Racial Disparities in COVID-19

gy, March 5, 2021.

27   Ashwini Deshpande, "How India's Caste Inequality Has Persisted—and Deepened in the Pandemic," *Current History*, April 1, 2021.

28   Daniel Hopkins, *The Greatest Killer: Smallpox in History*, 2002.

29   Nirenberg, op. cit.

30   Stephen Mihm, "The Ugly History of Blaming Ethnic Groups for Disease Outbreaks," *The Japan Times*, February 20, 2020.

31   Hays, op. cit., p. 113.

32   George Dillard, "What the Yellow Fever Epidemic of 1793 Revealed About America," *Lessons from History*, March 26, 2020.

33   Mary E. Fissell, "Pandemics Come and Go. The Way People Respond to Them Barely Changes," *The Washington Post*, May 7, 2020.

34   Hays, op. cit., p. 224.

35   Manuel Eisner and Amy Nivette, *Violence and the Pandemic: Urgent Questions for Research*, 2020.

36   Snowden, *Naples in the Time of Cholera, 1884-1911*, op. cit., p. 281. The term "Gypsy" is used here as it was used by Italian officials and the population at the time and as it appears in subsequent histories of these events.

37   Hays, op. cit., p. 334.

38   W. J. Simpson, "Recrudescence of Plague in the East," *Journal of the Sanitary Institute*, Vol. 20, Part IV, January 1900.

39   Steven Johnson, *The Ghost Map: The Story of London's Most Terrifying Epidemic and How It Changed Science, Cities, and the Modern World*, 2006, pp. 132-133.

40   Loomis, op. cit., pp. 251–252.

41   Sonia Scheer and David Holthouse, "Swine Flu Prompts Anti-Mexican Sentiment," *The Intelligence Report*, August 30, 2009.

42   Shawn Smallman, "Whom Do You Trust? Doubt and Conspiracy Theories in the 2009 Influenza Pandemic," *Journal of International and Global Studies*, Vol. 6, No. 2, April 2015.

43   Hilary Hylton, "Calls to Shut U.S.-Mexico Border Grow in Flu Scare," *Time*, April 29, 2009.

44   Camilo Montoya-Galvez, "What is Title 42, the COVID-19 border policy set to end in late May?" *CBS News*, April 5, 2022.

45   Mark Harrison, "'The Tender Frame of Man': Disease, Climate, and Racial Difference in India and the West Indies, 1760–1860," *Bulletin of History of Medicine*, Vol. 70, Issue 1, Spring 1996.

46   Erick Trickey, "Inside the Story of America's 19th Century Opiate Addiction," *Smithsonian Magazine*, January 4, 2018.

47   Carol Graham, *America's Crisis of Despair: A Federal Task Force for Economic Recovery and Societal Well-Being*, 2021; see also Anne Case and Angus Deaton, *Deaths of Despair and the Future of Capitalism*, 2020.

48   Michael S. Pollard, Joan S. Tucker, and Harold D. Green, Jr., "Changes in Adult Alcohol Use and Consequences During the COVID-19 Pandemic in the US," *JAMA Network*, September 29, 2020.

49   Joan B. Trauner, "The Chinese as Medical Scapegoats in San Francisco, 1870-1905," *California History*, Vol. 57, No. 1, Spring 1978.

50   Ibid.

51 Chase, op. cit., p. 106, citing Walter Wyman, *The Bubonic Plague*, 1900.
52 Becky Little, "Trump's 'Chinese' Virus Is Part of a Long History of Blaming Other Countries for Disease," *Time*, March 20, 2020.
53 Antonio Lillo, "COVID-19, the Beer Flu: Or, the Disease of Many Names," *De Gruyter Mouton*, October 28, 2020.
54 Alexandra Kelley, "Anti-Asian Hate Crimes Have Surged Nearly 150 Percent in Major U.S. Cities," *The Hill*, March 11, 2021.
55 Masood Farivar, "Attacks on Asian American Spiked by 164% in First Quarter of 2021," *Voice of America News*, April 30, 2021.
56 Center for the Study of Hate and Extremism, *Fact Sheet: Anti-Asian Hate Crime Reported to Police in America's Largest Cities: 2019 & 2020*, undated.
57 Carl Samson, "Mental Illness is 'Common Denominator' in Some Anti-Asian Attacks, NYPD Task Force Chief Says," *Yahoo News*, May 14, 2021.
58 Associated Press, "San Francisco reports major rise in anti-Asian hate crimes," *NBC News*, January 26, 2022.
59 "Alan Kraut Interview (excerpted)," *PBS*, undated.
60 Alan M. Kraut, "Immigration, Ethnicity, and the Pandemic," *Public Health Reports*, 2010.
61 Barry, *The Great Influenza*, op. cit., p. 395.
62 Erik Ortiz, "Racial Violence and a Pandemic: How the Red Summer of 1919 Relates to 2020," *NBC News*, June 21, 2020.
63 Cindy Alexander, *Statistics: Immigration in America, Ku Klux Klan Membership, 1840-1940*, undated, citing Kenneth T. Jackson, *The Ku Klux Klan in the City*, 1967.
64 Anti-Defamation League, *Antisemitic Incidents Hit All-Time High in 2019*, ADL Press Release, May 12, 2020.
65 European Union Agency for Fundamental Rights, *Antisemitism: Overview of Antisemitic Incidents Recorded in the European Union, 2009–2019*, undated.
66 Mitchell D. Silber, "Terrorist Attacks Against Jewish Targets in the West (2012–2019): The Atlantic Divide Between European and American Attackers," *CTC Sentinel*, Vol. 12, Issue 5, May/June 2019.
67 Alyssa Weiner, "Global Trends in Conspiracy Theories Linking Jews with Coronavirus," *AJC Global Voice*, May 1, 2020.
68 Craig Allen et al., "The Coronavirus Is Devastating Israel's Ultra-Orthodox Communities," *The New York Times*, February 17, 2021.
69 Eva Illouz, "Black Death Weakened the Catholic Church. COVID-19 Will Do the Same for Israel's Rabbis," *Haaretz*, March 4, 2021.
70 Cantor, op. cit.
71 Snowden, *Naples in the Time of Cholera, 1884-1911*, op. cit.
72 Oliwia Kowalczyk et al., "Religion and Faith Perception in a Pandemic of COVID-19," *Journal of Religion and Health*, No. 9, December 2020.
73 Andrew Cunningham, "Epidemics, Pandemics, and the Doomsday Scenario," *Historically Speaking*, September–October 2008.
74 Public Religion Research Institute, "The Coronavirus Pandemic's Impact on Religious Life," September 17, 2020; see also Christian Jouret, "How Religious Beliefs Have Responded to the Challenge of Covid-19," *Orient XXI*, April 17, 2020.

75 Mark Kreidler, "No major religious denomination opposes vaccination, but religious exemptions may still complicate mandates," *CNN News*, September 9, 2021.

76 Children's Health Defense—California Chapter, "Guide to Writing Religious Exemption Requests to CV-19 Vaccines."

77 Public Religion Research Institute, op. cit. As an example, according to the Public Religion Research Institute's poll of perceptions of the coronavirus as a critical issue, 79 percent of Black Protestants, 72 percent of Hispanic Catholics, 70 percent of those subscribing to non-Christian religions, and 66 percent of those unaffiliated with any religion assessed COVID-19 as the number one issue. In contrast, the pandemic did not make the top three critical issues listed by White Evangelical Protestants. Instead, abortion was the number one issue, followed by "fairness of presidential elections" and terrorism. In a June 2020 poll, 72 percent of White Evangelical Protestants were supporters of President Trump, and eight in ten said they would vote for him. Michael Lipka and Gregory A. Smith, "White Evangelical Approval of Trump Slips, but Eight-in-Ten Say They Would Vote for Him," Pew Research Center, July 1, 2020. This is not intended as a political commentary; it merely shows the coincidence of religious and political views.

78 Charles Gregg, "The Plague Mentality," *New Internationalist*, March 5, 1987.

79 Sarah Newey, "Conspiracy of Pandemics Past: The History of Disease and Denial," *The Telegraph*, November 5, 2020.

80 Ainsley Hawthorn, "Here's Why Disease Outbreaks Create Perfect Conditions for the Rise of Conspiracy Theories," *CBC*, November 8, 2020.

81 Maria Cohut, "The Flu Pandemic of 1918 and Early Conspiracy Theories," *Medical News Today*, undated.

82 Associated Press, "Conspiracy Theorists Are Burning 5G towers, Claiming They Are Linked to Coronavirus," *Los Angeles Times*, April 21, 2020.

83 Bethany Dawson, "Michael Flynn doubles down on conspiracy theory that COVID-19 was created by George Soros, Bill Gates, and WHO to steal the 2020 election from Trump," *Insider,* January 30, 2022.

84 Mark Hay, "The Shady Site That Shows Anti-Vaxxers Will Believe Anything," *Daily Beast*, January 22, 2022.

85 AT News Team, "Poll Indicates Large Numbers of Americans Think the World Is in the Biblical 'End Times,'" *AdventistToday.org*, September 12, 2013.

86 Pew Research Center, *More Americans Than People in Other Advanced Economies Say COVID-19 Has Strengthened Religious Faith*, January 27, 2021.

87 Paul A. Djupe, "The Political Implications of End Times Belief," *Religion in Public*, June 11, 2020.

88 Michael Durey, *The Return of the Plague: British Society and the Cholera, 1831–2*, 1979.

89 John M. Barry, "1918 Revisited: Lessons and Suggestions for Further Inquiry," *The Threat of Pandemic Influenza: Are We Ready? Workshop Summary*, 2005.

90 Arnstein Aassve et al., *Epidemics and Trust: The Case of the Spanish Flu*, March 2020.

91 Ibid.

92 Ibid.

93 For observations about declining civility in American society, see John Strausbaugh, "Have Our Manners Gone To Hell," *American Heritage*, September 1991, which was written 30 years ago; and *Civility in America: A Nationwide Study*, 2010.

94 Robin Blades, "The Psychological Toll of the Pandemic: What Isolation Does to the Brain," *Think Global Health*, November 23, 2020; Samuel Langton, "Lockdown Crime Trends: Why Antisocial Behavior Is Up," *The Conversation*, June 12, 2020.

95 Remi Jedwab et al., "Epidemics, pandemics, and social conflict," *World Development*, Vol. 147, July 17, 2021; Robert M. Sapolsky, "Double-Edged Swords in the Biology of Conflict," *Frontiers in Psychology*, December 20, 2018.

96 Thucydides, op. cit., Book II, Chapter 7; see also Gary Bass, "The Athenian Plague, a Cautionary Tale of Democracy's Fragility," *The New Yorker*, June 10, 2020.

97 Cantor, op. cit.; Samuel K. Cohn, Jr., "The Black Death: End of a Paradigm," *The American Historical Review*, Vol. 107, No. 3, 2002; Herlihy, op. cit. (the introduction by Samuel Cohn is especially useful); Kelly, op. cit.

98 Arnold, op. cit., p. 258.

99 Steven Stack and R. H. Rockett, "Social Distancing Predicts Suicide Rates: Analysis of the 1918 Flu Pandemic in 43 Large Cities, Research Note," *Suicide and Life-Threatening Behavior*, February 2021.

100 I. M. Wasserman, "The Impact of Epidemic, War, Prohibition and Media on Suicide: United States, 1910-1920," *Suicide and Life-Threatening Behavior*, Summer 1992; see also Knute Berger, "Seattle Struggled with Suicide in Late Stages of the 1918 Flu," *Crosscut*, May 7, 2020.

101 Eisner and Nivette, op. cit.

102 German Lopez, "2020's Historic Surge in Murders, Explained," *Vox*, March 25, 2021.

103 Caroline Newman, "The pandemic is increasing intimate partner violence. Here is how health care providers can help," *UAB News*, October 26, 2021.

104 "U.S. Firearms Sales December 2020: Sales Increases Slowing Down, Year's Total Sales Clock in at 23 Million," *Small Arms Analytics*, January 5, 2021.

105 Lopez, op. cit.

106 Hina Alam, "COVID May Be Contributing to Increase in 'Random Assaults' in Vancouver, Experts," *Global News*, October 27, 2021.

107 U.S. Federal Aviation Administration, *Unruly Passengers*, November 8, 2021.

108 Lauren Meckler and Valerie Strauss, "Back to School Has Brought Guns, Fighting and Acting Out," *The Washington Post*, October 26, 2021.

109 Amy Rock, "Hospital Assaults Hit All-Time High in 2020, IAHSS Survey Finds," *Campus Safety*, November 12, 2021.

110 Martin Savidge and Maria Cartaya, "Americans Bought Guns in Record Numbers in 2020 During a Year of Unrest—and the Surge Is Continuing," *cnn.com*, March 14, 2021.

111 Philip Bump, "Few of the Deaths Linked to Recent Protests Are Known to Have Been Caused by Demonstrators," *The Washington*

Post, August 26, 2020.

112 BBC News, "Coronavirus: Pfizer Confirms Fake Versions of Vaccine in Poland and Mexico," April 22, 2021.

113 Michael R. Blood, "California: Criminal Rings Loot Billions in Jobless Funds," *AP News*, January 25, 2021.

114 Europol, *Beyond the Pandemic—How COVID-19 Will Shape the Serious and Organized Crime Landscape in the EU,* April 30, 2020.

115 United Nations Office on Drugs and Crime, *Impact of the COVID Crisis on Migrant Smuggling,* September 2020.

116 John P Sullivan and Robert J. Bunker (eds.), *COVID-19, Gangs, and Conflict,* 2020.

117 The term was coined by Eric Hobsbawm and is described in his 1969 book, *Bandits*.

118 Oskar Gustafson, "Social Banditry, Myth and Historical Reality: Conceptualizing Contemporary Albanian Organized Crime Against the Hajduks," *Semantics Scholar,* 2017.

CHAPTER FOUR: POLITICAL REPERCUSSIONS

1 Luke Glanville, "Retaining the Mandate of Heaven: Sovereign Accountability in Ancient China," *Journal of International Studies,* November 2010.

2 Francis Fukuyama, "The Pandemic and Political Order," *Foreign Affairs,* Vol. 99, No. 4, July/August 2020.

3 Henry Meyer, "Putin's Boasts About Covid-19 Safety Are Unraveling," *Bloomberg,* June 18, 2021.

4 Jack Dutton, "What Is Happening in Colombia? Protests Against Ivan Duque Explained," *Newsweek,* May 4, 2021.

5 BBC News, "Why Colombia's Protests Are Unlikely to Fizzle Out," May 31, 2021.

6 James Westfall Thompson, "The Plague and World War: Parallels and Comparisons," in William M. Bowsky (ed.), *The Black Death: A Turning Point in History?* 1971.

7 Evans, *Death in Hamburg: Society and Politics in the Cholera Years,* op. cit., p. 385.

8 Snowden, *Naples in the Time of Cholera, 1884–1911,* op. cit., p. 366.

9 Ibid., p. 367.

10 Edward Cody, "Riots Follow Liberalization in Haiti," *The Washington Post,* June 13, 1984.

11 Evans, *Death in Hamburg: Society and Politics in the Cholera Years,* op. cit., p. 567.

12 Economist Intelligence Unit, "Democracy Index 2020: In sickness and in health," 2021. Seven democratic countries did extremely well with COVID-19 mortality rates less than half of the world average: Norway, Iceland, New Zealand, Finland, Australia, Japan, and South Korea—four of them are islands.

13 Sarita Santoshini, Ana Ionova, and Sara Miller Llana, "Global Populism: Big Promises, Poor Pandemic Results," *The Christian Science Monitor,* April 30, 2021.

14 Brian Dolan, "Commentary: Plague in San Francisco," 1900, 2006.

15 U.S. Department of Homeland Security, "National Terrorism Advisory System Bulletin," August 13, 2021.

16   Richard S. Ross, III, *Contagion in Prussia, 1831: The Cholera Epidemic and the Threat of the Polish Uprising*, 2015, p. 246.

17   Ibid, p. 247.

18   Samuel K. Cohn, Jr., "Popular Insurrection and the Black Death: A Comparative View," *Past & Present*, Vol. 195, Issue suppl. 2, 2007.

19   Ibid.

20   Ibid.

21   Mark Bailey, *After the Black Death: Economy, society, and the law in fourteenth century England*, 2021.

22   John Ashton, "COVID-19 and the Summer of Blood of 1381," *Journal of Royal Society of Medicine*, Vol. 113, No. 10, (1990); Dan Jones, *Summer of Blood: England's First Revolution*, 2009; W. M. Ormrod, "The Peasants Revolt and the Government of England," *Journal of British Studies*, Vol. 29, No. 1 (January 1990); Dylan Vosti, *Concerning Peasants: The Underlying Cause for the Peasants' Revolt of 1381*, 2017.

23   George A. Holmes, "England: A Decisive Turning Point" in William M. Bowsky (ed.), *The Black Death: A Turning Point in History?* 1971.

24   Bailey, *After the Black Death*, op. cit.

25   Samuel K. Cohn, Jr., "Cholera Revolts: A Class Struggle We May Not Like," *Social History*, Vol. 42, Issue 2, 2017, p. 166.

26   Ibid., pp. 162–163.

27   Durey, op. cit., p. 184.

28   Cohn, "Cholera Revolts: A Class Struggle We May Not Like," op. cit., p. 166.

29   Ibid, pp. 165–166.

30   Durey, op. cit., p. 184.

31   Evans, *Death in Hamburg: Society and Politics in the Cholera Years*, op. cit., p. 477.

32   Evans, "Epidemics and Revolutions: Cholera in Nineteenth Century Europe," op. cit.

33   Ibid.

34   Snowden, *Naples in the Time of Cholera, 1884-1911*, op. cit.

35   Although he does not specifically address the cholera riots, British historian Eric Hobsbawm theorized that early lawbreakers were actually primitive revolutionaries. See Hobsbawm, *Social Bandits and Primitive Rebels*, 2000 (originally published in 1969).

36   Daniel Pick, *Faces of Degeneration: A European Disorder, c. 1848-c. 1918*, 1989, p. 14.

37   Ibid., p. 21.

38   Spinney, op. cit., p. 253.

39   Ibid., pp. 250–252.

40   Barry, *The Great Influenza*, op. cit., p. 394.

41   Plato, *Republic*, Volume II, Book 6, Loeb Classical Library, Christopher Emlyn-Jones (ed.), William Preddy (translator), 2013.

42   Anja Steinbauer, "The Ship of Fools," *Philosophy Now*, Issue 101, March/April 2014.

CHAPTER FIVE: EPIDEMICS AND ARMED CONFLICT

1   Joan Evans, *Life in Medieval France*, 1925.

2   Dave Roos, "How 5 of History's Worst Pandemics Finally Ended,"

History, March 4, 2021.

3   Cohn, "The Black Death: End of a Paradigm," op. cit., pp. 703–738.
4   James C. Davies, "Toward a Theory of Revolution," *American Sociological Review*, Vol. 27, No. 1, February 1962.
5   Ted Robert Gurr, *Why Men Rebel*, 1970; see also Gurr, "Why Men Rebel Redux: How Valid Are its Arguments 40 Years On?" *E-International Relations*, November 17, 2011.
6   Kenneth Letendre et al., "Does Infectious Disease Cause Globalization in the Frequency of Intrastate Armed Conflict and Civil War?" *Global Innovation Index*, 2020.
7   Soumitra Dutta et al. (eds.), "Interactive Database of the GII Indicators: Political and Operational Stability," *Global Innovation Index*, 2020.
8   Celina Menzel, *The Impact of Outbreaks of Infectious Diseases on Political Stability: Examining the Examples of Ebola, Tuberculosis and Influenza*, 2018.
9   Jedwab, et al., op.cit.
10 Hays, op. cit., pp. 494–500.
11 Andrew Price-Smith, *The Health of Nations: Infectious Disease, Environmental Change, and Their Effects on National Security and Development*, 2002, p. 16.
12 Nicolas Van de Walle, "The Health of Nations: Infectious Disease, Environmental Change, and Their Effects on National Security and Development," *Journal of Interdisciplinary History*, Vol. 34, No. 1, Summer 2003.
13 Andrew Price-Smith, *Contagion and Chaos: Disease, Ecology, and National Security in the Era of Globalization*, 2009, p. 16.
14 Matteo Cervellati, Uwe Sunde, and Simona Valmori, *Disease Environment and Civil Conflicts*, 2021.
15 Ibid.
16 Stewart Patrick, *Weak Links: Fragile States, Global Threats, and International Security*, 2011, p. 207.
17 Katariina Mustasilta, *From Bad to Worse? The impact(s) of Covid-19 on Conflict Dynamics*, 2020.
18 BBC News, "Coronavirus: Five of the Countries Most at Risk from Famine in 2020," April 22, 2020.
19 Mustasilta, op.cit.
20 Lazar Berman and Jennifer Tischler, "After the Calamity: Unexpected Effects of Epidemics on War," *RealClearDefense*, June 30, 2020.
21 Daniel Richter, "War and Culture: The Iroquois Experience," *The William and Mary Quarterly*, Vol. 40, No. 4 (October 1983); J. Norman Heard, "Captives of American Indians," *Handbook of Texas*, undated.
22 Ilkka Syvanne, *Military History of Late Rome—518-565*, 2021. p. 365.
23 William Rosen, *Justinian's Flea: The First Great Plague and the End of the Roman Empire*, op. cit.
24 Richard Gunderman, "How Smallpox Devastated the Aztecs—and Helped Spain Conquer an American Civilization," *PBS Newshour*, February 23, 2019; Sarah Roller, "The Worst Epidemic in History? The Scourge of Smallpox in the Americas," *History HIIT*, October 6, 2020.
25 The letters were preserved as part of the British Manuscript Project undertaken by the U.S. Library of Congress, where they can be viewed on microfilm. See *Jeffrey Amherst and Smallpox Blankets: Lord Jeffrey*

Amherst's letters discussing germ warfare against American Indians.

26 William C. Summers, *The Great Manchurian Plague of 1910–1911: The Geopolitics of an Epidemic Disease*, 2012.

27 David E. Sanger and Anton Troianovski, "U.S. Intelligence weighs Putin's two years of extreme pandemic isolation as a factor in his wartime mind-set," *The New York Times*, March 5, 2022.

28 Jonathan Tepperman, "Putin in His Labyrinth: Alexander Gabuev on the View from Moscow," *The Octavian Report*, March 14, 2022.

29 Tanya Lewis, "How the War in Ukraine is Causing Indirect Deaths," *Scientific American*, March 29, 2022.

30 Vikram Mittal, "The Impact of the COVID-19 Pandemic on Russian Operations in Ukraine," *Forbes*, March 17, 2022.

31 United Nations Office for the Coordination of Humanitarian Affairs, "Attacks on Ukraine's Hospitals Will Cause Long-Term Harm to Health," *reliefweb*, March 22, 2022.

32 Annie Sparrow et al., "Cholera in the time of war: implications of weak surveillance in Syria for the WHO's preparedness—a comparison of two monitoring systems," *BMJ Global Health*, 2016.

CHAPTER SIX: POST-PANDEMIC TERRORISM

1 Jing-Bao Nie, "In the Shadow of Biological Warfare: Conspiracy Theories on the Origins of COVID-19 and Enhancing Global Governance of Biosafety as a Matter of Urgency," *Journal of Bioethical Inquiry*, August 25, 2020.

2 Daniel M. Gerstein, "Origin Story: How Did the Coronavirus Emerge?" *The National Interest*, June 2, 2021.

3 David Rapoport, "Four Waves of Modern Terrorism" in John Horgan and Kurt Braddock (eds.), *Terrorism Studies: A Reader*, 2008.

4 McGrew, op. cit., p. 154.

5 Snowden, *Epidemics and Society: From the Black Death to the Present*, op. cit., p. 235.

6 Tom Goyan, "Road to Notoriety: Johann Most in Austria (1868–1871)," *Journal for the Study of Radicalism*, Vol. 12, No. 2, Fall 2018.

7 *The Anarchists Versus the Plague: Malatesta and the Cholera Epidemic of 1884*, CrimethInc., undated.

8 Andrew T. Price-Smith presents an excellent discussion about this phenomenon in *Contagion and Chaos: Disease, Ecology, and National Security in the Era of Globalization*, op. cit.

9 Anton Gollwitzer et al., "Partisan Differences in Physical Distancing Are Linked to Health Outcomes During the COVID-19 Pandemic," *Nature Human Behavior*, November 2, 2020.

10 U.S. Department of Justice, "Six Arrested on Federal Charge of Conspiracy to Kidnap the Governor of Michigan," *Justice News*, October 8, 2022.

11 Mitch Smith, "Two Men Acquitted of Plotting to Kidnap Michigan Governor in High-Profile Trial," *The New York Times*, April 8, 2022.

12 Reuters, "German police detain four over alleged plot to kidnap health minister," *The Guardian*, April 14, 2022.

13 Cheryl Teh, "A GOP Candidate in Pennsylvania Called for '20 Strong Men' to Remove School Boards that Impose Mask Mandates on Students," *Business Insider*, August 31, 2021.

14 Julian Mark, "Tennessee Parents Make Threats After School Board Mandates Masks: 'We Will Find You,'" *The Washington Post*, August 12, 2021.
15 Peter Hotez, "COVID Vaccines: Time to Confront Anit-Vax Aggression," *Nature*, April 27, 2021.
16 Christian Johnson and William Marcellino, *Bad Actors in News Reporting: Tracking News Manipulation by State Actors*, 2021.
17 Jari Tanner, "Russia Hopes to Use COVID-19 to Weaken Western Unity, Intel Report Claims," *The Times of Israel*, February 11, 2021; see also: Michael R. Gordon and Dustin Volz, "Russian Disinformation Campaign Aims to Undermine Confidence in Pfizer, Other Covid-19 Vaccines, U.S. Officials Say," *The Wall Street Journal*, March 7, 2021.
18 Ibid.
19 Nelson Oliveira, "Man Drives into Workers at COVID Vaccination Clinic During Brazen Attack in California," *New York Daily News*, August 23, 2021.
20 U.S. Department of Homeland Security, *Summary of Terrorism Threat to the U.S. Homeland,* August 13, 2021.
21 Tavis Bohlinger, "The Covid Vaccine has 666 Written All Over It . . . and Why That Doesn't Matter According to Revelation," *The Lab*, May 18, 2020; see also Elizabeth Dwoskin, "On Social Media, Vaccine Misinformation Mixes with Extreme Faith," *The Washington Post*, February 16, 2021.
22 Rapoport, op. cit.
23 Max Roser et al., "War and Peace," Our World in Data, 2016.
24 U.S. Secretary of Defense Jim Mattis, "Summary of the National Defense Strategy of the United States of America: Sharpening the American Military's Competitive Edge," January 19, 2018.
25 Thomas S. Szayna et al., "What Are the Trends in Armed Conflicts, and What Do They Mean for U.S. Defense Policy?" 2017.
26 Brian Michael Jenkins, "The Future Role of the U.S. Armed Forces in Counterterrorism," *CTC Sentinel*, Vol. 13, Issue 9, September 2020.
27 "Leon Trotsky Quotes," *Goodreads*, undated.
28 Louis Beam, "Leaderless Resistance," 1983, republished in *The Seditionist*, 1992.
29 Michelle Harven, "What Is Anarchism?" *WAMU NPR*, October 12, 2020.
30 United Nations Security Council, Counter-Terrorism Committee Executive Directorate, "Update of the COVID-19 pandemic on terrorism, counter-terrorism, and countering violent extremism, June 2021," June 2021; updated December 2021,

CHAPTER SEVEN: THE PANDEMIC AND BIOTERRORISM

1 John Horgan, "The Plague at Athens," *World History Encyclopedia,* August 24, 2016.
2 Manolis J. Papagrigorakis et al., "The plague of Athens: an ancient act of bioterrorism," *Biosecur Bioterror,* Vol. 11, Issue 3, September 2013.
3 Stefan Riedel, "Biological warfare and bioterrorism: a historical review," *Baylor University Medical Center Proceedings*, Vol. 17, Issue 4, (October 2004); see also: H. J. Jansen et al., "Biological warfare, bioterrorism, and biocrime," *Clinical Microbiology and Infection*, Vol. 20, Issue 6, June 2014; Brad Roberts (ed.) *Terrorism With Chemical and*

Biological Weapons: Calibrating Risks and Responses, 1997; and Jessica Stern, *The Ultimate Terrorists*, 1999.

4   Cited in Helena Costa and Josep-E Baños, "Bioterrorism in the Literature of the Nineteenth Century: The Case of Wells and *The Stolen Bacillus*," *Cogent Arts & Humanities*, Vol. 3, Issue 1, August 9, 2016.

5   Michael Miner, "The Terrorist Mind—A Look Back at a 1972 Plot to Poison Chicago," *Chicago Reader*, September 25, 2012; see also W. Seth Carus, "R.I.S.E. (1972)" in Jonathan B. Tucker (ed.), *Toxic Terror: Assessing Terrorist Use of Chemical and Biological Weapons*, 2000.

6   Hiroshi Takahashi et al., "Bacillus Anthracis Bioterrorism Incident in Kameido, Tokyo, 1993," *Emerging Infectious Diseases*, Vol. 10, No. 1, January 2004; see also Kyle B. Olson, "Aum Shinrikyo: Once and Future Threat?" *Emerging Infectious Diseases*, Vol. 5, No. 4, August 1999.

7   Rebecca Frerichs et al., "Historical Precedence and Technical Requirements of Biological Weapons Use: A Threat Assessment," 2004.

8   Robert J. Lifton, *The Broken Connection*, 1979.

9   Sammy Salama and Lydia Hansell, "Does Intent Equal Capability? Al-Qaeda and Weapons of Mass Destruction," *Nonproliferation Review*, Vol. 12, No. 3, November 2005.

10   Scott Decker, *Recounting the Anthrax Attacks: Terror, the Amerithrax Task Force, and the Evolution of Forensics in the FBI*, 2018.

11   Frerichs et al., op. cit., p. 46.

12   John Parachini, *Combating Terrorism: Assessing the Threat of Biological Terrorism*, 2001.

13   "President Bush Delivers Graduation Speech at West Point," June 1, 2002.

CHAPTER EIGHT: LOOKING AHEAD

1   Horrox, op. cit., p. 230; McNeill, op. cit., p. 191.

2   *Washington Post-University of Maryland Poll*, conducted December 17-19, 2021.

3   Francis Oakley, *The Crucial Centuries: The Medieval Experience*, 1979, pp. 41-42.

4   Pew Research Center, "83% Say Measles Vaccine Is Safe for Healthy Children," February 9, 2015.

5   Aaron Blake, "Here's how many Americans are actually anti-vaxxers," *The Washington Post*, February 9, 2015.

6   Kaia Hubbard, "Fewer Americans Than Ever Before Against Vaccinations," *U.S. News & World Report*, August 31. 2021.

7   Pew Research Center, "83% Say Measles Vaccine Is Safe for Healthy Children," op.cit.

8   Jennifer Kates, Jennifer Tolbert, and Anna Rouw, "The Red/Blue Divide in COVID-19 Vaccination Rates: An Update," *KFF*, January 19, 2022.

9   Lydia Saad, "More in U.S. Vaccinated After Delta Surge, FDA Decision," *Gallup*, September 29, 2021.

10   Bump, op. cit.

11   Geoff Brumfiel, "What's Driving the Political Divide Over Vaccinations," *NPR*, December 9, 2021.

12   ACASignups.net, "Weekly Update: #COVID-19 Case/Death Rates By County, Partisan Lean & Vaccination Rate," December 2, 2021.

13   Kattie Mettler et.al., "Anti-vaccine activists march in D.C.—a city that mandates coronavirus vaccination—to protest mandates," *The Washington Post*, January 23, 2022.

14   Nell Clark, "The Ottawa trucker protest is rooted in extremism, a national security expert says," *NPR*, February 10, 2022.

15   Annalisa Merelli, "The average anti-vaxxer is probably not who you think she is," *Quartz*, March 4, 2015.

16   Nicole Lyn Pesce, "This is the most anti-vaxxer country in the world," *Market Watch*, June 19, 2019.

17   Rob Picheta, "Europe's loud, rule-breaking unvaccinated are falling out of society," *CNN.com*, January 16, 2022.

DRAMATIS PESTILENTIAE

1   Cohn, *Epidemics: Hate and Compassion from the Plague of Athens to AIDS*, op. cit., p. 11.

2   Kyle Harper, *The Fate of Rome: Climate, Disease, and the End of an Empire*, 2019.

3   History.com Editors, *Cholera*, updated March 24, 2020.

4   Reginald Farrar, *Plague in Manchuria*, October 27, 1911.

FOR A FULL LIST OF WORKS CONSULTED, PLEASE VISIT:

https://www.mhpbooks.com/books/plagues-and-their-aftermath/

ABOUT THE AUTHOR

BRIAN MICHAEL JENKINS is a senior advisor to the president of the RAND Corporation. He served in the U.S. Army's Special Forces during the war in Vietnam, before joining RAND in 1972. In 1996, President Bill Clinton appointed Jenkins to the White House Commission on Aviation Safety and Security. Jenkins has also served as advisor to the National Commission on Terrorism. He is a frequent commentator on matters of global security and safety for major media outlets including NBC, PBS, NPR, *The New York Times*, *The Washington Post*, and others.